THE NAVIGATOR BIBLE STUDIES HANDBOOK

THE NAVIGATOR BIBLE STUDIES HAND-BOOK

NAVPRESS

A MINISTRY OF THE NAVIGATORS

P.O. Box 6000, Colorado Springs, Colorado 80934

The Navigators is an international Christian organization. Jesus Christ gave His followers the Great Commission to go and make disciples (Matthew 28:19). The aim of The Navigators is to help fulfill that commission by multiplying laborers for Christ in every nation.

NavPress is the publishing ministry of The Navigators. NavPress publications are tools to help Christians grow. Although publications alone cannot make disciples or change lives, they can help believers learn biblical discipleship, and apply what they learn to their lives and ministries.

© 1975 by The Navigators
Revised Edition © 1979 by The Navigators
All rights reserved, including translation
Library of Congress Catalog Card Number: 79-87654
ISBN: 0-89109-075-4
10751

Eleventh printing, 1986

Unless otherwise identified, all Scripture quotations are from the *Holy Bible: New International Version* (NIV). Copyright © 1973, 1978, 1984, International Bible Society. Used by permission of Zondervan Bible Publishers. Other versions quoted are the *King James Version* (KJV); *The New American Standard Bible* (NASB), © The Lockman Foundation 1960, 1962, 1963, 1968, 1971, 1972, 1973, 1975, and 1977; and the *Williams New Testament* by Charles B. Williams (WMS), © 1937, 1965, 1966 by Edith S. Williams. Moody Bible Institute of Chicago. Used by permission.

Printed in the United States of America

CONTENTS

My son, if you accept my words
and store up my commands within you,
turning your ear to wisdom
and applying your heart to understanding,
and if you call out for insight
and cry aloud for understanding,
and if you look for it as for silver
and search for it as for hidden treasure,
then you will understand the fear of the Lord
and find the knowledge of God.

Proverbs 2:1-5

INTRODUCTION

MANY Christians are discovering that the Bible is an open, exciting book whose truths, like valuable gems, enrich their lives. Yes, you can do inductive Bible study yourself in your own home! But the key to doing it is being systematic and consistent.

Your personal Bible study week by week with the self-help methods presented in this book will build and establish you in your knowledge of the Bible, help you maintain fellowship with Jesus Christ, and equip you to teach others. Then as you faithfully apply the Word of God to your life, your study will help you conform more and more to the character of Christ. This goal alone is worth the discipline of time and effort your study requires each week. Resolve now to let nothing keep you from regular, personal Bible study.

Solomon urged us to search the Word of God as for hidden treasure, as we would seek for silver—the treasures of wisdom, knowledge, and understanding (see Proverbs 2:1-5). Jesus, speaking of the Scriptures, said, "These are the Scriptures that testify about Me" (John 5:39), and also affirmed, "Everything must be fulfilled that is written about Me in the Law of Moses, the Prophets and the Psalms" (Luke 24:44). He endorsed the testimony that He is revealed in all the Bible, and confirmed to us the central motive for Bible study—*coming to know Him better.*

The two units in this handbook are:

- *The Basics of Bible Study,* which will give you important background information for all the methods of Bible study.
- *Types of Bible Studies,* which will teach you some of the time-tested methods of Bible study The Navigators have used in past decades.

UNIT ONE
THE BASICS
OF BIBLE STUDY

KNOW YOUR GOAL

GOD wants every believer to be like His Son, Jesus Christ. Paul wrote, "Those God foreknew He also predestined to be conformed to the likeness of His Son" (Romans 8:29). The transformation of your life into the likeness of Jesus Christ will enable you to join in fulfilling creation's eternal purpose—to glorify the Creator.

Conformity to Christ is a lifelong process which is completed only when you pass into God's presence. Paul described this process: "All of us, with faces uncovered, because we continue to reflect like mirrors the splendor of the Lord, are being transformed into likeness to Him, from one degree of splendor to another, since it comes from the Lord who is the Spirit" (2 Corinthians 3:18, WMS).

Bible study is a vital part of this process. If you will study God's Word faithfully, pray for understanding, and diligently apply the Scriptures to your experience and daily walk, your life will change and increasingly glorify God.

Many spiritual truths have thought-provoking parallels in the physical world. Take, for example, a thirsty person coming to a well. Before he can quench his thirst, he must let down the bucket, draw the water, and then take a drink.

God's Word is able to satisfy the spiritually dry and thirsty person, even as Jesus promised "living water" to the woman by the well in Samaria. First, however, he must study the Bible to draw out its truths, then personally apply them to his own life.

Drawing the water compares to the academic study of God's Word. Good study methods and habits help us toward proper understanding and application of Scripture. The Apostle Paul wrote to a co-worker, "Do your best to present yourself to God as one approved, a workman who does not need to be ashamed and who correctly handles the word of truth" (2 Timothy 2:15).

Drinking the water compares to believing and applying God's Word. James stated, "The man who looks intently into the perfect law that gives freedom, and continues to do this, not forgetting what he has heard, but doing it—he will be blessed in what he does" (James 1:25).

THE CHARACTERISTICS OF BIBLE STUDY

Personal Bible study that is life-changing is not something done haphazardly. A study that is meaningful, applicable, and life-affecting will have the following five main characteristics.

It Must Be Systematic and Consistent

Jesus explained the Scriptures systematically (Luke 24:27), and the Berean Jews evaluated the Gospel they heard by its consistency with Scripture (Acts 17:11). Your study must also be systematic and consistent. R. A. Torrey, great Bible teacher of another generation, advised, "Have some good system of Bible study and follow it. System counts in everything, but it counts more in study than in anything else, and it counts more in Bible study than in any other form of study."*

---

*R. A. Torrey, *The Importance and Value of Proper Bible Study* (Chicago: The Bible Institute Colportage Association, 1921), p. 54.

It Must Be Original Investigation in the Bible Itself

Personal Bible study does not depend on what others have said *about* the Scriptures, but must involve the student in the Bible itself. Again Torrey urges, "Do not study about the Bible; study the Bible."* Libraries of books have been written about the Bible, but there is only one Bible. So go to the source. As you study, compare Scripture with Scripture. One portion of it sheds light on another, enriching your Bible study experience and answering your questions.

It Must Be a Written Reproduction of Your Findings

An important part of the learning process is reproducing in your own words what you have studied. Dawson Trotman, founder of The Navigators, said, "Thoughts disentangle themselves passing over the lips or through the pencil tips." If you want to master the truths of Scripture, write them down in your own words.

It Must Be Personally Applied to Daily Living

You need to follow the psalmist's example when he wrote, "I thought on my ways, and turned my feet unto Thy testimonies. I made haste, and delayed not to keep Thy commandments" (Psalm 119:59-60, KJV). The Scriptures are the means by which the Holy Spirit changes our lives, but in this ministry He needs our cooperation.

It Must Be "Pass-on-able"

A good personal Bible study method is one that is simple enough to be easily passed on. Teaching someone else how to study the Bible for himself is far better than sharing what you have received from your own study, though that is helpful too. Solomon advised, "Drink water from your own cistern, running water from your own well" (Proverbs 5:15).

(These five characteristics of Bible study are from the ministry of Lorne C. Sanny, president of The Navigators.)

---

*Torrey, *Proper Bible Study*, p. 33.

AS YOU BEGIN

Good Bible study methods alone cannot guarantee a changed life. The Bible can only be understood fully with the aid of the Holy Spirit. Apart from a growing personal relationship with God, the academic study of the Word will produce little change. Some important steps of personal preparation are necessary.

A Cleansed Life

Refusing to deal with sin in your life breaks fellowship with God. The secret of restored fellowship and the cleansed life is very simple. John tells us what we should do: "If we confess our sins, He is faithful and just and will forgive us our sins and purify us from all unrighteousness" (1 John 1:9). Before beginning your Bible study, stop and confess to God any known sins.

Prayer for Illumination

Since understanding the Scripture can come only through the illuminating ministry of the Holy Spirit, you need to follow the example of the psalmist when he prayed, "Praise be to You, O Lord; teach me Your decrees. . . . Open my eyes that I may see wonderful things in Your law. . . . Let me understand the teaching of Your precepts; then I will meditate on Your wonders. . . . Direct me in the path of Your commands, for there I find delight" (Psalm 119:12, 18, 27, 35).

Dependence on the Holy Spirit

One of the Holy Spirit's ministries is to teach Christians the truths from the Bible. Jesus promised, "The Counselor, the Holy Spirit, whom the Father will send in My name, will teach you all things and will remind you of everything I have said to you" (John 14:26). Paul declared, "We have not received the spirit of the world but the Spirit who is from God, that we may understand what God has freely given us" (1 Corinthians 2:12). You must rely on His instructions, following Solomon's wise advice, "Trust in the Lord with all your heart and lean not on your own understanding" (Proverbs 3:5).

Willingness to Obey

Jesus pointed out that a prerequisite to knowing the truth is willingness to obey the truth. "If any one chooses to do God's will, he will find out whether My teaching comes from God or whether I speak on My own" (John 7:17). The one who is willing to obey will receive God's instruction.

YOUR APPROACH

THE conclusions you draw from your study will reflect your basic beliefs about the Bible. Three fundamental beliefs lead to proper understanding of Scripture.

BASIC BELIEFS

The Bible Is the Literal Word of God

The Apostle Paul stated categorically, "All Scripture is inspired by God" (2 Timothy 3:16, NASB). This statement is foundational to Bible study. Because the Bible is God's inerrant communication to men, it deserves careful study and investigation.

The Bible is literal in the sense that its accounts are records of actual happenings, not a collection of myths and legends. The writers of Scripture, however, do at times use figurative statements, allegories, and symbols.

The Bible Is God's Means of Revealing Truth to His People

Man alone cannot discover God's plans; God must reveal them. His truth is not revealed in the silent contemplation of your own life or of nature around you, but through the Holy Spirit's illumination of the inspired Word. Jesus taught, "If you hold to My teaching, you are really My disciples. Then you will know the truth, and the truth will set you free" (John 8:31-32).

The Bible Is Authoritative

The Bible has authority because God is its author and has absolute authority over men. Every area of every man's life is subject to the Word of God. During His temptation Jesus declared, quoting the Old Testament, "Man does not live on bread alone, but on every word that comes from the mouth of God" (Matthew 4:4; see Deuteronomy 8:3).

KEEPING ON TRACK

In order to handle the Word of God properly, it is important to follow certain guidelines of interpretation (*hermeneutics* is the academic word). Observing these guidelines does not always guarantee correct conclusions, but disregarding them frequently leads to error.

Walt Henrichsen has written a helpful book on this subject: *A Layman's Guide to Interpreting the Bible* (NavPress, 1979). The rules he suggests are summarized below. You would profit greatly by also reading the explanations and examples of these given in his book.

General Principles of Interpretation

1. Work from the assumption that the Bible is authoritative.
2. The Bible interprets itself; Scripture best explains Scripture.
3. Saving faith and the Holy Spirit are necessary for us to understand and properly interpret the Scriptures.
4. Interpret personal experience in the light of Scripture and not Scripture in the light of personal experience.
5. Biblical examples are authoritative only when supported by a command. *A corollary*: The believer is free to do anything that the Bible does not prohibit.
6. The primary purpose of the Bible is not to increase our knowledge but to change our lives. *Two corollaries*:

    a. Some passages are not to be applied in the same way they were applied at the time they were written.

    b. When you apply a passage, it must be in keeping with a correct interpretation.

7. Each Christian has the right and responsibility to investigate and interpret the Word of God for himself.

8. Church history is important but not decisive in the interpretation of Scripture. *A corollary*: The Church does not determine what the Bible teaches; the Bible determines what the Church teaches.

9. The promises of God throughout the Bible are available to the Holy Spirit for the believers of every generation.

Grammatical Principles of Interpretation

1. Scripture has only one meaning and should be taken literally.

2. Interpret words in harmony with their meaning in the times of the author.

3. Interpret a word in relation to its sentence and context.

4. Interpret a passage in harmony with its context.

5. When an inanimate object is used to describe a living being, the statement may be considered figurative. *A corollary*: When life and action are attributed to inanimate objects, the statement may be considered figurative.

6. When an expression is out of character with the thing described, the statement may be considered to be a figurative one.

7. The principal parts and figures of a parable represent certain realities. Consider only these principal parts and figures when drawing conclusions.

8. Interpret the words of the prophets in their usual, literal, and historical sense, unless the context or manner in which they are fulfilled clearly indicates they have a symbolic meaning. Their fulfillment may be in installments, each fulfillment of prophecy being a pledge of that which is to follow.

Historical Principles of Interpretation

1. Since Scripture originated in a historical context, it can be understood only in the light of biblical history.
2. Though God's revelation in the Scriptures is progressive, both Old and New Testaments are essential parts of this revelation and form a unit.
3. Historical facts or events become symbols of spiritual truths only if the Scriptures so designate them.

Theological Principles of Interpretation

1. You must understand the Bible grammatically before you can understand it theologically.
2. A doctrine cannot be considered biblical unless it sums up and includes all that the Scriptures say about it.
3. When two doctrines taught in the Bible appear to be contradictory, accept both as scriptural in the confident belief that they resolve themselves into a higher unity.
4. A teaching merely implied in Scripture may be considered biblical when a comparison of related passages supports the teaching.

STEPS FOR CHANGING YOUR LIFE

I N order to achieve the final goal of a changed life, it is important to know how to make good personal applications from Scripture. The essential steps in this process are observation, interpretation, then application.

Observation

Observation is the act of seeing, taking notice of things as they really are—the art of awareness. Observation depends on two root attitudes: an open mind and a willing spirit.

Sometimes people approach Bible study with preconceived notions. Their attitude often is, "Don't confuse me with the facts; my mind is made up!" An open mind is necessary for effective Bible study. A willing spirit is necessary because whenever you guard an area of your life, you hinder understanding. The man who is unwilling to be changed in his marriage will not even see his needs as a husband. The woman who refuses to admit to vanity in her life will probably not see it condemned in the Scriptures.

Accurate observation is the result of reading with diligence, purposefulness, thoughtfulness, and inquiry. Reading till the Word jogs the mind and heart requires quality time. As you study, read for the message, not for mileage.

> *"Observation demands concentration! The purpose of observation is to saturate yourself thoroughly with the content of a passage. Like a sponge you should absorb everything that is before you."* —Oletta Wald* .

You will learn more if you record what you observe. As you write down your thoughts, they become clearer. Get a study Bible in which you can underline important words, write in the margins, and draw arrows to connect associated terms. Be sure to define important words and phrases. Without knowing the meaning of words, it is hard to understand the truths of the Bible. One of the best reference books for Bible study is a dictionary.

Six important questions will help you make accurate observations.

Who?	— Who are the people involved?
What?	— What happened? What ideas are expressed? What are the results?
Where?	— Where does this take place? What is the setting?
When?	— When did it take place? What was the historical period?
Why?	— Why did it happen? What is the purpose? What is the stated reason?
How?	— How are things accomplished? How effectively? By what method?

Interpretation

Interpretation, the step of determining the author's meaning, seeks to clarify the meaning of a passage and help you understand why the Holy Spirit included this portion in Scripture. Interpretation answers the question, "What does it mean?"

The Bible is the literal Word of God and means what it

---

*From *The Joy of Discovery* by Oletta Wald, Copyright 1956 by Bible Banner Press, Minneapolis, Minnesota. Used by permission.

says. However, there is often more than one definition of a word. Correct interpretation depends on determining the definition the writer had in mind.

One aspect of interpretation is correlation—the process of relating the passage under consideration to the rest of the chapter, the whole book, and other portions of Scripture. This prevents forcing a meaning on a passage which was not intended by the writer. Since the Bible is truth and all truth is unified, all interpretations must be consistent and coherent with the rest of the Bible.

One word of warning: The human mind cannot understand all that God has revealed. When established teachings in the Scripture appear contradictory, both truths should be accepted in the confident belief that they will resolve themselves into a higher unity. How Jesus could be both fully man and fully God is difficult to understand. It must, however, be accepted and believed.

It is important to look for the paragraph divisions in a passage and consider each verse in light of its relationship to the paragraph as a whole. Sometimes a paragraph may overlap a chapter division. In that case, disregard the chapter division.

Application

Application is putting God's Word into practice in your life—recognizing in the Scriptures their personal message to you and responding accordingly. The psalmist wrote, "I have considered my ways and have turned my steps to Your statutes. I will hasten and not delay to keep Your commands" (Psalm 119:59-60).

The benefit of Bible study is not derived from methods, techniques, or diligent efforts to decipher the text. The benefit is in obeying the voice of the Lord—receiving what He says and putting it into practice. Application doesn't happen by osmosis or by chance; application is by intent.

Application starts with the willing acceptance of truth. A right response to Scripture is characterized by trust, obedience, praise, and thanksgiving. The application may include remembering an impressive truth, changing a wrong attitude, or taking a positive action.

Respond to God, not a rule book! Responses should be motivated by love. The goal is to glorify God by pleasing Him in every area of life. Unwillingness to apply the Scriptures personally inevitably leads to spiritual insensitivity to the Lord and to people.

The following five questions—which can be remembered by the acronym SPECK—can help you apply the Word to your life:

S —Is there a *sin* for me to avoid?
P —Is there a *promise* from God for me to claim?
E —Is there an *example* for me to follow?
C —Is there a *command* for me to obey?
K —How can this passage increase my *knowledge* about God or about Jesus Christ?

An Example of Essential Steps

Consider how these vital elements of Bible study might be used in studying Paul's statement to the church at Thessalonica: "Because our gospel came to you not simply with words, but also with power, with the Holy Spirit and with deep conviction. You know how we lived among you for your sake" (1 Thessalonians 1:5).

Observation: The Gospel Paul preached to the Thessalonians had a greater effect than mere words; the Thessalonians were aware of the kind of life Paul lived.

Interpretation: Paul's exemplary life was one reason why the Gospel had power. The Holy Spirit gave power to his words and enabled him to live that kind of life. (Correlation: Paul later states that the Thessalonians knew about his holiness, righteousness, and blamelessness [1 Thessalonians 2:10].)

Application: I need to concentrate on living a life of holiness as I tell others of Jesus Christ. In particular, I need to correct my critical attitude toward those who are not immediately receptive to what I say.

SUMMARY OF UNIT ONE

Know Your Goal

1. The objective of Bible study is to glorify God as you change into a more Christlike person.

2. The Characteristics of Bible Study
   a. It must be systematic and consistent.
   b. It must be original investigation in the Bible itself.
   c. It must be a written reproduction of your findings.
   d. It must be personally applied to daily living.
   e. It must be "pass-on-able."

3. As You Begin
   a. A cleansed life.
   b. Prayer for illumination.
   c. Dependence on the Holy Spirit.
   d. Willingness to obey.

Your Approach

1. Basic Beliefs
   a. The Bible is the literal Word of God.
   b. The Bible is God's means of revealing truth.
   c. The Bible is authoritative.

2. Keeping on Track
   Twenty-four rules of interpretation taken from Walt Henrichsen's *A Layman's Guide to Interpreting the Bible*.

Steps for Changing Your Life
1. Observation
2. Interpretation
3. Application

UNIT TWO
TYPES
OF BIBLE STUDIES

NOTE

For the seven Bible study methods described in Chapters 6 through 12, two things have been included in this book to help you get the most out of using these methods:

(1) Following page 108 in the back of the book are blank, printed forms for each of the seven methods. These pages are perforated, and can be detached and machine-copied as often as you like.

(2) At the end of each chapter is a sample study showing the method described in that chapter. The sample shows how you can use the Bible study method on blank notebook paper, writing in your own headings for the various sections of the study.

BIBLE STUDY
FOR A LIFETIME

THE Apostle Paul exhorted Timothy, "Do your best to present yourself to God as one approved, a workman who does not need to be ashamed and who correctly handles the word of truth" (2 Timothy 2:15). The person who studies the Word of God diligently is a workman—he is learning to handle the Word correctly and he stands approved before God. He is called a workman because it takes work to study. Many Christians do not study the Scriptures because it involves work, discipline, and precious time. But for those who are willing to make the effort, their study will be well worthwhile.

Bible study is an essential part of a Christian's life; in fact, a person who would be a disciple of the Lord Jesus Christ must be doing personal Bible study. It is one of the major means of becoming Christlike—of building biblical qualities into a Christian's life.

But there is a great difference between merely *doing* Bible study, which can be drab and perfunctory, and *studying* the Bible in a way which is exciting and life-changing. The real goal of Bible study is to see our lives changed to be more like Jesus Christ's.

Bible study should therefore be a lifetime project. In each

stage of a Christian's spiritual development he should be engaged in life-changing, applicatory study of the Scriptures. To do this, he should begin with simple methods of study, and move into more advanced ones later for a change of pace.

This unit presents eight methods of Bible study that have been used successfully by The Navigators for many years, including the well-known question-and-answer method. The normal progression is to begin with question-and-answer types of Bible study, then move into analytical methods. As a Christian matures spiritually, analytical study should become his lifetime intake of the Word of God. The seven methods described in Chapters 6 to 12 give specific instructions on how to do analysis types of study.

The chart on page 31 shows the progression of Bible study methods described in Chapters 5 through 12. These steps need not be followed in the sequence shown, but the chart does present a logical progression. For variety, you may want to frequently change to different methods.

- *Stage 1.* Here the new Christian or one who has never done Bible study begins with simple question-and-answer studies. The Navigators recommend *Lessons on Assurance* or *Lessons on Christian Living*.
- *Stage 2.* He then moves into advanced question-and-answer studies—preferably the *Design for Discipleship* series or the *Studies in Christian Living*—or Verse Analysis (Chapter 6).
- *Stage 3.* The next step might be the ABC Bible Study (Chapter 7), a simple chapter analysis approach that helps establish Bible study habits. Another option is the *Scripture Memory Study Plan*, which combines Bible study and Scripture memory by examining analytically the context of a verse being memorized.
- *Stage 4.* This stage adds another option suitable for Bible study—the Search the Scriptures study (Chapter 8), an analytical approach to the books of the Bible. Also, the Topical Bible Study (Chapter 11) and

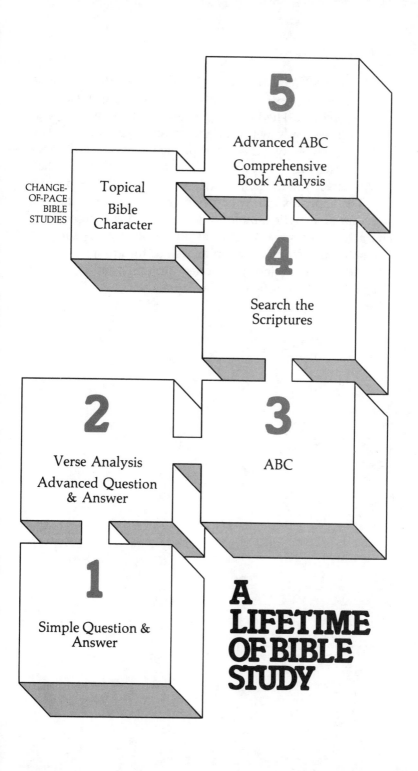

5

Advanced ABC

Comprehensive
Book Analysis

CHANGE-
OF-PACE
BIBLE
STUDIES

Topical

Bible Character

4

Search the
Scriptures

2

Verse Analysis

Advanced Question
& Answer

3

ABC

1

Simple Question &
Answer

A LIFETIME OF BIBLE STUDY

Bible Character Study (Chapter 12) are change-of-pace suggestions at this stage or in the fifth stage.

- *Stage 5.* The last stage continues lifetime analytical Bible study with the options of the Advanced ABC Bible Study (Chapter 9) or the Comprehensive Book Analysis (Chapter 10). The topical and Bible character studies continue to serve as changes of pace.

The appendix following Chapter 12 suggests a nine-year program of analytical Bible study combined with topical and character studies. This serves as an excellent guide for your personal Bible study program as well as for groups.

All the materials mentioned in this chapter and in Chapter 5 are published by NavPress.

QUESTION & ANSWER BIBLE STUDIES

QUESTION-and-answer Bible studies are the most popular approach to studying the Scriptures, and for good reason. The question-and-answer format is easily understood, so that Bible studies of this kind serve especially well as an introduction to the Scriptures for new and growing Christians. And by touching on a variety of topics throughout the Bible in a relatively short time, these studies can build a foundation for understanding major scriptural teachings.

The question-and-answer format can also be used in advanced Bible study courses, such as *The Life and Ministry of Jesus Christ*. But let us look first at an elementary course—*Lessons on Assurance*. This booklet has five lessons, each one beginning with questions based on five key verses or passages on assurance, which are to be memorized. These verses deal with a Christian's assurance of salvation, answered prayer, victory over sin, forgiveness, and guidance from God. Each lesson also includes several other questions based on a variety of verses scattered throughout both the Old and New Testaments.

Continuing in the same format is the Navigator booklet *Lessons on Christian Living*. Its eight chapters allow the student to examine several crucial foundations of the Christian life. Here again the student memorizes and meditates on key verses, and looks up several others to answer further questions about the topic. Both here and in *Lessons on Assurance*, the lessons conclude with a section for the student to write down a way of applying to his life the scriptural truths he has just learned.

Two larger question-and-answer study series are *Studies in Christian Living* and *Design for Discipleship*. The basic format remains the same—questions are asked, appropriate Scripture passages are given for the student to research his answers, and space is provided in the booklet for writing in the answers. However, the questions in these courses—particularly in *Design for Discipleship*—are more probing and require more thought before answering.

Both courses concentrate on giving the student a deeper understanding of the truths and practical principles of discipleship. *Design for Discipleship* is somewhat more advanced and proceeds at a faster pace, while *Studies in Christian Living* is particularly helpful for those with less scriptural background.

Studies in Christian Living is a nine-booklet set. The first booklet has three chapters which are well-suited for an evangelistic Bible study for non-Christians. (These chapters, which examine the person and work of Jesus Christ and contain a clear presentation of how to become a Christian, can also be obtained as three separate leaflets.) The next five booklets in the course include 23 chapters on basic discipleship topics, while the last three booklets introduce a different method of Bible study—chapter analysis.

Design for Discipleship offers thirty-six chapters in seven booklets. The first six booklets include thought-provoking questions about scriptural issues. The seventh booklet introduces chapter analysis through a study of 1 Thessalonians.

Both series are used mainly in informal, small discussion groups. Participants complete the lessons on their own before meeting together. One chapter a week is the usual pace, and application is emphasized.

Topics studied include the authority of the Bible, servanthood, purity of life, the lordship of Christ, world vision, and several others.

On a still more difficult level is *The Life and Ministry of Jesus Christ*. This comprehensive examination of the four Gospels in harmony form asks questions that require extensive study of the Scriptures, and often the use of outside sources as well. Consisting of three books with six chapters each, the series progresses chronologically from Old Testament prophecies of Christ's coming through Jesus' birth, ministry, death, resurrection, and ascension.

Included in the books are maps, an ongoing harmony of the Gospels, and several excerpts from scholarly accounts of the cultural, historical, and geographical background of Christ's life on earth. Detailed instructions explain the various parts of the study.

Since the primary goal of Bible study is to change your life, the chapters in *The Life and Ministry of Jesus Christ*, as well as those in *Studies in Christian Living* and *Design for Discipleship*, include sections for applying to your life the truths learned in your study.

HOW TO DO VERSE ANALYSIS

VERSE Analysis is a rewarding place to begin analytical Bible study. The instructions are simple. First, copy the verse from one or more versions of the Bible. Write it under the heading VERSE FOR STUDY.

Then, under the heading MESSAGE, write out in your own words what the verse says—what it commands, teaches, warns of, or promises.

Now look at the verses immediately preceding and following the verse. These are known as the *context* of the verse. Under the heading CONTEXT, record first the thoughts added by the verses preceding your study verse. Then record the thoughts added by the verses following the study verse.

Record next the questions that the verse raises in your mind, or the problems you think it might pose for yourself or someone else. These can be recorded under the heading QUESTIONS.

The final section of your study is the APPLICATION. Under this heading you should describe one specific way you can change your attitudes or actions because of the teaching of this verse.

VERSE FOR STUDY: Philippians 4:11
"Not that I speak in respect of want; for I have learned,
in whatever state I am, in this to be content."

MESSAGE:
It teaches that Paul had to learn to be content.
Contentment is not based on what you have or don't have.
Circumstances are a tool in God's hands, not for making
me content, but for making me more like Jesus Christ.

CONTEXT:
Philippians 4:10 — Paul did have needs which the Philippians
were helping him in. But it was precisely from these needs
that Paul was free — emotionally, spiritually, and
psychologically.
Philippians 4:12-13 — It is not only in want that we need
to be content — but in plenty as well. Then we are
totally free and uncontrolled by the circumstances
of life and the things of this world, and are able to be
secure, and to find our happiness, joy, peace, and
contentment solely in Jesus Christ — because He is my
life and the length of my days (Deuteronomy 30:20).
In Him I live and move and have my being (Acts 17:28)

(AN EXAMPLE OF VERSE ANALYSIS)

QUESTIONS:

How do I <u>learn</u> contentment?

If contentment is not based on what I have or don't have, on what <u>is</u> it based?

What exactly does it mean to be content?

What are some clues for identifying discontentment?

APPLICATION:

To be content in the unknowns of life — the future that is always unseen — to know that I need only Jesus for this day, and that I can always know Him, even if I don't know the future. Since circumstances are only a <u>tool</u> in God's hands, I need to yield myself to this tool to become what God intends for me to become. In my new job which I begin next week, I have anxiety about whether I will really like it. But today I will thank God for that job, since He arranged for me to have it, and I will decide to enjoy my being there.

(AN EXAMPLE OF VERSE ANALYSIS)

CHAPTER SEVEN

HOW TO DO THE ABC BIBLE STUDY

"**W**HEN Your words came, I ate them," wrote the Prophet Jeremiah. "They were my joy and my heart's delight, for I bear Your name, O Lord God Almighty" (Jeremiah 15:16). Today, centuries later, personal Bible study allows us to experience the joy and delight in God's Word which Jeremiah spoke of.

The ABC Bible Study plan is one of the most basic tools for analytical Bible study, and gives the Holy Spirit opportunity to speak to you directly from the Scriptures. It is best in this basic Bible study format not to refer to commentaries or other reference materials. Learn to glean truth from the Scriptures on your own. You may refer to other reference materials later.

Getting Started

Review Unit One in this handbook, *The Basics of Bible Study*, then choose a passage or chapter from a New Testament book for your study. Before you do any writing, prayerfully read the chosen study portion at least three times. You may read it silently, then aloud, then pausing to reflect at the end of each verse on what you have read.

It is better to do the entire ABC study in rough draft

form first. Then organize it neatly under the five following sections, each identified by a letter of the alphabet. The sections need not be done in the order shown.

A. A Title

You may want to write your title after you have finished the rest of your study. In choosing a title, jot down two or three titles that come to mind as you study; then either select the best one from this list or form a new one from a combination of your suggestions. The title should fit the chapter and be as complete as possible.

Your aim is to look for a title that clearly identifies the passage's content, not for one that is catchy. It should not exceed 11 words and may be just one or two.

B. Best Verse or Basic Passage

Decide whether you are choosing a Best Verse or a Basic Passage. Write the reference of the verse or verses under the section heading.

The Best Verse is a single reference that seems most outstanding to you as you read through the passage or chapter, even though it may not contain the central theme. The Basic Passage is a verse or group of verses (no more than three) which includes the central message or is the key to the contents of the passage.

C. Challenge

As you work through the passage this time, ask God to challenge your heart in a personal way from some portion of what you are studying. Your purpose now is to *accept* this challenge and *apply* its truth in a definite way to your life. It may be something that God wants you to do or stop doing, or an attitude to develop. A habit may need to be formed or broken. You may need to incorporate some truth into your thinking.

Under the heading CHALLENGE, begin with the number of the verse or verses from which you are taking your challenge. First state *in your own words* the truth of the verse. Then tell how this challenge applies to you—what needs it reveals in your life, what shortcomings, transgressions, or neglects it indicates, or what new appreciation or understanding it opens up to you. Since the challenge is personal, use the pronouns "I," "me," "my," and "mine" in your writing.

Then state clearly what you plan to do about it. Tell what specific action you will take to correct the weakness, to build the needed quality into your life, or to increase your understanding of this truth. Choose something practical you can do in the following week, instead of a long-term project. Your next Bible study will bring another challenge that you will want to work on.

This action step may be one of many things, such as writing a letter, memorizing a verse of Scripture on the subject, praying about a special need, doing a kindness, making an apology and asking forgiveness, or carrying out a short-term project. Remember to depend on the Holy Spirit, who enables us to truly grow in our Christian life.

D. *Difficulties*

Consider each verse in your study passage. Does it speak of anything you could not explain to another person? If so, under the heading DIFFICULTIES write down the number of the verse and the question or problem it raises in your mind. Do not merely say, "I don't understand" or "Please explain," but state the specific difficulty it presents to you.

If a difficulty can be answered by a little research (such as looking up a word in a dictionary), do the research and record the answer. Then you can share it with someone in your discussion group who might have a similar question.

E. *Essence*

In the last section of your study, you may choose to *summarize* or *outline* the passage under the heading ESSENCE. In either case, you should record only what the passage *says*, not what it *means*. Rather than interpreting it, simply put in your own words what the Scripture actually says.

The *summary* is a brief condensation of the passage. You should summarize all parts of the passage equally, not giving too much space to one part and slighting another. One way to do this is to write one sentence in your rough draft for each successive thought in the passage, using your own words instead of the words of the text. Then condense your summary into fewer words, combining your sentences and making them shorter. You should aim for an average of two to eight words per verse.

An *outline* divides a passage into its natural paragraphs and gives a brief title or heading to each section. Write down the verses included in each section (see below). List as many subpoints under each of the main headings as you need to define its content. As in the summary, include all parts of the passage in good proportion. An outline may look like this:

    I. Main Heading or Title of This Division (1:1-8)
       A. Subpoint (verses 1-3)
       B. Subpoint (verses 4-8)
    II. Main Heading or Title of This Division (1:9-21)
       A. Subpoint (verses 9-10)
       B. Subpoint (verses 11-16)
          1. Sub-subpoint (verses 11-13)
          2. Sub-subpoint (verses 14-16)
       C. Subpoint (verses 17-21)

A Final Word

Again, your ABC Bible Study should include the following parts:

      A TITLE
      BEST VERSE or BASIC PASSAGE
      CHALLENGE
      DIFFICULTIES
      ESSENCE

BOOK: Colossians   STUDY PASSAGE: 3:1-11

A. TITLE:
The Christian's New Life

B. BEST VERSE: Colossians 3:3

C. CHALLENGE:
VERSE OF THE CHALLENGE: Colossians 3:2
TRUTH OF THE CHALLENGE: My mind is to be
occupied with godly thoughts and desires, not wanting
what the world has to offer.
PERSONAL APPLICATION OF THE CHALLENGE: It's easy
to think I must have certain things or live a certain way in
the world's eyes to be happy. The world's propaganda
seems to get to me. Then I get anxious when I don't
get these things. This verse reminds me I need to
set my mind to think God's way with God's values.
This happens only as my mind is filled with His Word.
I need to develop the habit of meditating on Scripture.
This week I'll take one verse I have memorized and
concentrate on using it to meditate on all week.
I'll use 1 Corinthians 15:58.

(AN EXAMPLE OF THE ABC BIBLE STUDY)

D. DIFFICULTIES:

Vs.	Difficulties
1	How has the Christian been raised with Christ?
	What are the "things above" I am to seek?
2	How do I "set" my mind?
5	How can I "put to death" my earthly nature?
	Do I do this actively, or does God bring it about
	in my life?
10	Why is it necessary to have my new nature
	"renewed in knowledge"?

E. ESSENCE:

The Christian's New Life (Colossians 3:1-11)

I. Centered in Christ (1-4)

A. Raised with Christ

  1. Seek things above (1)

  2. Set my mind on things above (2)

B. Appearing with Christ

  1. I have died—my life is hidden with Christ (3)

  2. I will appear with Christ (4)

II. Contrast of old and new (5-11)

A. Old

  1. The old character—put it to death (5-6)

  2. Old practices—put them away (7-9)

B. New

  1. The new self—in God's image (10)

  2. No partiality in Christ (11)

(AN EXAMPLE OF THE ABC BIBLE STUDY)

CHAPTER EIGHT

HOW TO DO
SEARCH
THE SCRIPTURES

THE people of Berea were commended for receiving Paul's message "with great eagerness" and for the way they "examined the Scriptures every day to see if what he said was true" (Acts 17:11). The King James Version says they "searched" the Scriptures daily.

The words *examine* and *search* imply close inspection or methodical scrutiny, indicating that the Bereans took time to consider carefully and thoughtfully the content and meaning of God's written Word. They searched for the wisdom of God as for hidden treasure, even as Solomon exhorted many centuries before (Proverbs 2:4).

When you study God's Word with diligence and "great eagerness," the result is always well worth the effort. And the greatest personal benefit comes from completing your own study before referring to such outside helps as commentaries or notes by others. What you discover yourself is usually more exciting and valuable to you personally than the writings of godly men, even though the latter may be more scholarly.

Search the Scriptures is a flexible plan designed to meet the needs of people with varying abilities and amounts of time available for study.

Getting Started

Review Unit One in this handbook, *The Basics of Bible Study*, then choose a study portion. You may use the four-part Search the Scriptures study for an entire chapter of the Bible, a part of a chapter, a paragraph, or even a single verse. Each section in this plan represents a different way to consider the study passage.

If you decide to study a book chapter by chapter, you will find it helpful to do a book preview first, and a book summary at the end. Directions for doing a preview and a summary are on pages 49-51.

Do the study in rough draft form first. Then organize it neatly in final form, using the following headings.

Point of the Passage

This part of your study asks the question, "What does this passage say?" When studying the Scriptures, it is important that you read carefully *what is written*. This is the *observation* essential of Bible study (pages 20-21). Notice first the passage's actual content rather than trying to interpret its meaning. In this section of your study, you will *summarize* or *outline* what the text actually says.

First, read the passage a number of times with definite goals in mind. In your first reading, try to grasp the main thoughts of the passage; this will enable you to divide the passage into smaller logical units. Then reread each unit to gain more detail about the main thought of that section.

After your reading, if you choose to write a *summary*, write perhaps one sentence for each separate thought of the study passage, using your own words. Now read your summary to see if you have included all the parts of the passage in proper balance, not giving too much space to one part and overlooking another.

Go through your summary and condense it, combining and restating until the content of the passage is briefly and clearly stated *in your own words*. A good summary will average two to eight words per verse. The purpose of condensing and rewriting your summary is to help you get a better grasp of the content of the chapter or portion.

If you prefer to write an *outline*, read the Scripture portion carefully as you would for a summary. Then divide the passage into its natural divisions or paragraphs and give each part a brief title or heading. Write the verse numbers of each section at the end of the heading. List as many subpoints under each of these main headings as you need to outline the content clearly. Do not give too much space to one part of the passage and overlook another; include *all* the important points. The main headings should be somewhat similar in form; subpoints should also have some regularity and each should relate to the main point it is under.

Parallel Passages

This section asks the question, "What does it say elsewhere in Scripture about the points in this passage?" The best commentary on the Bible is the Bible itself. You will best understand a portion of Scripture as you allow other passages to throw light on it. A good practice is to compare thoughts and ideas gleaned from one portion of Scripture with what is said in others. This broadens your perspective on each subject.

Read each verse carefully, then meditate on it and try to remember one or more good cross-references for that particular passage. These may be drawn from verses you have memorized or from familiar chapters. If your memory fails to lead you to a good cross-reference, use a concordance or the marginal notes in your Bible to find one. It is important to try to cross-reference the thought of the verse rather than select verses that merely use an identical word. Choose passages that support the thought by adding information, giving an example, or revealing a different viewpoint.

Use the subheadings REFERENCE and KEY THOUGHT in this section. Write down the reference of the parallel passage and the key thought or idea that connects the parallel passage with the verse you are cross-referencing. This will enable you to refer quickly to all your parallel passages.

It is not necessary to cross-reference all verses in the chapter; try to get cross-references for at least all the outstanding verses.

Problems of the Passage

This section asks the question, "What does it say that I don't understand?" Read through the passage slowly this time to see if you could explain everything and answer any questions you might be asked about it. If questions or problems come to mind, write these down. Write the verse number before each question and state the problem clearly and briefly. State specifically what is not understood; do not list a reference and simply add "I do not understand" or "Please explain."

You may find problems in the study portion that you could answer, but which might not be clear to a person younger in years or in spiritual understanding. After you have listed the problems that *you* could not answer fully, list these *possible* problems and mark them as such.

Profit of the Passage

This final section asks the question, "What does it say to *me*?" Applying the Scriptures to daily living is the most important result of Bible study. It provides you with practical ways to glorify the Lord in your everyday life, and is a stepping-stone to greater fruitfulness. James said we deceive ourselves if we hear the Word and do not do it (James 1:22).

Your profit should be drawn from a verse or group of verses that concern *one* particular thought. You will benefit more from developing one serious, specific application than from merely mentioning several challenges. Indicate the verse number at the beginning as you write it.

Write your application on either your relationship to God or your relationship to others. In other words, your application should result in your personal spiritual enrichment either by deepening your devotion to the Lord or by improving your relationship to fellow Christians or to persons outside of Christ. You may draw your application from a promise, a command, or some truth that speaks to your heart as you prayerfully consider the portion for study.

When you write, use the pronouns "I," "me," and "mine." Your application should be *practical* and should concern a truth you can translate into daily living. State it clearly enough to be understood by anyone you might ask to read it.

You may want to write your profit in three parts:

1. State *in your own words* the truth of the verse from which you are drawing your application, that is, what the Scriptures teach that you should be, think, or do.

2. Indicate how it applies to you—what need it brings out in your life, where you fall short, and what new appreciation or understanding it gives.

3. Write what you intend to do about it—what definite action you will take to correct the weakness, build the needed quality into your life, or strengthen your understanding. This step of action may be memorizing a verse on the subject, doing a special Bible study on it, or praying about a need. It may be writing a letter of apology, righting some wrong you have done, or doing some kindness. Whatever action is needed, be as specific as you can about what you intend to do and then make a provision to carry it out. It is also a good idea to provide yourself with a future reminder to make sure you have followed through on your action.

To make your applications more effective, share them with one or more friends to gain their prayer support and encouragement.

If you decide to study an entire book using the Search the Scriptures plan, follow the complete procedure as explained above for each chapter before proceeding to the next chapter.

Book Preview and Book Summary

As an option for a thorough study of an entire book of the Bible, it is helpful to do a book preview during the first week of your study and a book summary the last week, after you have gone through the book chapter by chapter.

Book Preview—Here are four steps to follow in your book preview:

1. Read the book through in one sitting.

2. Get background information on the book, using the notes and maps in your Bible or in a Bible handbook. Consult a reliable Bible dictionary or encyclopedia if necessary. Find the following information:

   a. Who wrote the book?
   b. When and where was it written?
   c. To whom was it written?
   d. Why was it written? What was the writer's purpose in writing? What problem was it meant to solve or what main instruction does it give?
   e. What information do the Gospels or the Book of Acts give on this book or its writer, if any? (A concordance will help you trace references to the writer or to the places involved.)

3. Read the book again and list one or more main themes of the book. Try to discover these on your own before consulting outside helps.

4. Write a brief personal application on some portion of the book.

Book Summary—Follow these seven steps for your book summary:

1. Review your book preview.

2. Read the book through again once or twice. Read quickly and try to get the sweep of the whole book.

3. Outline or summarize the entire book, using your POINT OF THE PASSAGE sections from each chapter as guides.

4. List your PROFIT OF THE PASSAGE from each chapter by using a short, descriptive title or a two-line summary.

5. Reread the book, referring to your summary or outline (Item 3 above) as you read.

6. Write a title for the book. Try to make it identify the contents of the book.

7. List the main lessons and challenges you received from the book. Spend some time reviewing and praying over these challenges, and write out any further action you need to take during the coming week.

Summary

Again, the headings you should include in a Search the Scriptures study are:

      POINT OF THE PASSAGE (summary or outline)
      PARALLEL PASSAGES (cross-references)
      PROBLEMS OF THE PASSAGE (questions)
      PROFIT OF THE PASSAGE (application)

Your study may also include a book preview and a book summary.

Group Use of Search the Scriptures

When the Search the Scriptures study is used with a group that includes people of different backgrounds and varying degrees of spiritual maturity and time for study, it is best to go through a book of the Bible, assigning a chapter at a time. Some will be able to study the entire chapter according to the Search the Scriptures plan. Others who have less time for study or less background in personal Bible study can use the Search the Scriptures method on the portion of the chapter they consider most important. This portion may include a few verses, half the chapter, or even more. Another alternative is for the whole group to decide to do the study on a single key verse or selected portion of the chapter.

With this flexibility in the group Bible study plan, no one should have to come to a group discussion without *some* work done. It is *very important* that those doing the Search the Scriptures study do some preparation before the group meets each time, whether it is on the entire chapter, a group of verses, or the key verse. Steady progress of this sort builds habits that will soon enable the serious student to finish an entire chapter each time.

STUDY PASSAGE: 1 John 3:11-24 (14 verses)

POINT OF THE PASSAGE:

We have been taught to love each other. This is one way we can tell if we have eternal life — if our actions are loving and righteous. Of course the world will hate us; that's why Cain killed Abel.

Love is Jesus dying for us, and He is our example. This love demands action on our part, such as meeting our brother's needs. This love is not just words.

Loving actions will lead to peace of mind and a clear conscience, and a clear conscience leads to confidence before God. This confidence assures us of being in God's will and having our prayers answered.

The Holy Spirit reminds us of God's presence with us if we continue to have faith in Jesus, and love others.

PARALLEL PASSAGES:

vs.	Reference	Key Thought
11	John 13:34-35	We are commanded to love.
13	John 15:19	The world hates Christians.
14	John 13:35	Love is the test of new life.
15	Matthew 5:22	Hatred or anger with a brother is as bad as murder.
16	1 Thess. 2:8	Giving our lives for our brothers
17	James 2:15-16	We must meet our brothers' physical needs.
22	Hebrews 13:21	Our lives are to be pleasing in God's sight.

(AN EXAMPLE OF SEARCH THE SCRIPTURES)

23	John 6:29	We are commanded to believe in Jesus.
24	Romans 8:9	The Holy Spirit is proof of God's
		presence.

PROBLEMS OF THE PASSAGE:

Vs.	Question
13	Why does the world hate us?
18	Can we also truly express love with our speech?
20	What does it mean for our hearts to condemn us? When do our hearts condemn us?
22	How do I really determine what is pleasing in God's sight?

PROFIT OF THE PASSAGE:

Verses 18 and 19 say that our confidence and assurance depend on our obedience to God's command to love others in deed and truth. My many anxious moments and doubts are therefore directly traceable to my lack of giving and doing for others.

I intend within the next week to give an entire evening to my children to do "their thing", and one night to my wife at her favorite restaurant.

(AN EXAMPLE OF SEARCH THE SCRIPTURES)

CHAPTER NINE

HOW TO DO THE ADVANCED ABC BIBLE STUDY

THE Advanced ABC Bible Study plan allows you to develop the same study methods introduced in the Search the Scriptures and ABC Bible Study plans. It also allows you to crystallize what you are learning by stating the eminent truth in your study passage. Use the Advanced ABC method to study an entire book, chapter by chapter.

Getting Started

Review Unit One in this handbook, *The Basics of Bible Study*, then select a New Testament book for your Advanced ABC study. (Some Old Testament books, such as Jonah, Nehemiah, or Ruth, lend themselves to this method of study, but try them only after you have used Advanced ABC long enough to feel comfortable with it.)

One chapter a week is a good pace for most people. If a chapter is particularly long, however, you may decide to do it in two studies.

Ask the Holy Spirit of God to guide and enlighten you as you begin your study. Approach the Bible with a prayer like that of the psalmist, "Open my eyes that I may see wonderful things in Your law" (Psalm 119:18). A new experience in God's Word is waiting for you.

To get the greatest benefit from your study, you should do a book survey the first week and a book summary at the end of your chapter-by-chapter study. Directions for doing these are on pages 60-61.

You should read through the chapter slowly and prayerfully at least once as you start your study, then at least once aloud, and at least once pausing at the end of each verse to reflect on what you have read. (You may want to write down the number of times you have read the chapter in each of these ways.) Then work through the chapter again as you do each part of the study.

The Advanced ABC Bible Study has seven parts. Either the BASIC PASSAGE, CROSS-REFERENCES, or DIFFICULTIES sections would make a good place to start. You can do your TITLE, FINAL STUDY, EMINENT TRUTH, and APPLICATION more effectively after combing through the chapter verse by verse on some of the other sections.

Should you find you are using too much of your time on one section, such as CROSS-REFERENCES, it may be helpful to budget a certain amount of time for each section, and so be able to do some work on each part of the study before your available time is used up. (Some record should be kept of the approximate time spent in doing the study. Write this somewhere on your final study.)

As you are working on one section of your study, a good verse or idea might come to you regarding another section. Don't lose it, but jot it down on a separate sheet of paper and go back to the section you are working on.

It is best to do the study in rough draft form first. Then organize it neatly in final form.

Making Your Title Fit

In choosing a title, jot down on a separate sheet of paper two or three titles that come to mind as you study; then either select the best one from this list or form a new one from a combination of your suggestions. The title should fit the chapter and be as complete as possible.

Your aim is to look for a title that clearly identifies the chapter content, not for one that is catchy. It should not exceed 11 words and may be only one or two words long. You may want to choose your final title after completing the various parts of your study.

A. Application

Apply the Word of God to your life. Jesus told His disciples, "Now that you know these things, you will be blessed if you do them" (John 13:17). It is through putting into practice what we learn from God's Word that we are renewed in the attitude of our minds (see Ephesians 4:23) and transformed into godliness rather than being conformed to the pattern of this world (see Romans 12:2).

Your application will spell out some practical way you can glorify God by obeying His Word. It may speak of something God wants you to do or stop doing, some habit you need to form or break, or simply a new awareness of some truth to incorporate into your thinking.

Choose your application either *in relation to God* or *in relation to others*. In relation to God, your application may be an appreciation of some great truth which deepens your devotion to Him, leads to some needed correction in attitude, or strengthens or improves your fellowship with Him. It may also involve some promise or command that affects your relationship with Him. If your application is in relation to others, it will aim toward improving your relationship with fellow Christians or with those who do not know Jesus Christ. This type of application usually relates to your outreach and service for the Lord.

Begin with the number of the verse or verses from which you are taking your application. Then state *in your own words* the truth of the verse. Use the pronouns "I," "me," "my," and "mine" to make your application your own. Tell how the truth applies to you—what it reveals in your life, what shortcomings, transgressions, or neglect it indicates, or what new appreciation or understanding it opens up to you.

If possible, mention an incident in your life which illustrates the failure or need.

Then state clearly what you plan to do about this. Tell what specific action you will take to correct the weakness, to build the needed quality into your life, or to increase your understanding of this truth. Choose something practical that you can do within the following week, instead of a long-term project. Your next Bible study will bring a new application to work on.

The action step of an application may be one of many things, such as writing a letter, memorizing a verse of Scripture on the subject, praying about a special need, doing a kindness, making an apology and asking forgiveness, or taking a step toward forming or breaking a habit. You should also have a checkup plan to remind you to carry out your application. And remember that for every step of growth in your Christian life, you must depend on the Holy Spirit.

B. Basic Passage

In this part of your study, select the verse or verses (no more than three) containing the dominant theme of the chapter—the truth around which the chapter is centered. After reading through the chapter, start with verse one and consider whether it might be the basic passage. Continue through the chapter looking at each verse in this way. You may end up with several possible basic passages; eliminate all but your final choice.

In some chapters it will be impossible to select one key verse or passage, as in a chapter containing several parables or complete stories. You may then choose a key verse for each section, indicating the section first and then listing the basic passage for it.

C. Cross-references

The teaching on most subjects in the Bible is not found in complete form in a single chapter. It is good, therefore, to compare one portion of Scripture with another on the same subject, for the best commentary on the Bible is the Bible itself. You will best understand a portion of Scripture as you allow other passages to throw light on it, and this will expand your knowledge and perspective on a given topic.

Consider each verse or passage carefully, meditate on it, and then try to remember good cross-references for that particular section. These may be drawn from verses you have memorized or from familiar chapters. If one does not come to mind, use a concordance or marginal references in your Bible, selecting a cross-reference for the thought or subject rather than one which merely uses identical words. Choose cross-references that support the thought by adding information, giving an example, or revealing a different viewpoint.

Under the subheadings VERSE, CROSS-REFERENCE, and KEY THOUGHT, write the number of the verse in the chapter you are studying to which the cross-reference relates, the cross-reference, and two or three words giving the central thought which links the two verses together.

D. Difficulties

Difficulties and problems will arise as you go through the chapter. Keep asking yourself, "Does this verse speak of anything I could not explain to someone else?" If so, write down the verse number and the question or problem it raises in your mind. Do not merely say, "I do not understand" or "Please explain," but state your question clearly. This will free your mind for further investigation of the chapter.

Toward the end of your study you may want to look at your DIFFICULTIES section and answer some of the problems that could be solved by your research (such as consulting a Bible dictionary or handbook). When you find an answer, write it down. You will then be able to explain it to someone else who might have a similar question.

E. Eminent Truth

The EMINENT TRUTH section is a miniature topical or doctrinal study within the chapter. It should be the main teaching of the chapter, but may center in a small portion or a single verse. Your basic passage will often be the basis of the eminent truth.

Make your choice of the eminent truth by asking yourself, "Is this the *main* truth or spiritual principle the Holy Spirit is teaching in this chapter?" First state the truth, then develop it with various points from the rest of the chapter. As much as possible, document your statements with specific verses from within the chapter. You may also draw from other parts of the Bible to develop the eminent truth.

F. Final Study

In this section of your study, you will either summarize or outline the chapter. In either case, you will record only what the chapter *says*, not what it *means*, using the Bible study essential of *observation* (pages 20-21) rather than *interpretation*. This will enable you to put the actual content of the chapter into your own words.

For a *summary*, write a brief synopsis of the chapter. Be sure to include all parts of the chapter, not giving too much space to one part and slighting another. Write one sentence for each successive thought in the chapter, using your own words. Then condense your summary into fewer words, combining your sentences and restating more briefly. You should aim for an average of two to eight words per verse.

For an *outline*, divide the chapter into its natural sections or paragraphs and give a brief title or heading for each. Beside the title, note the verse numbers for that section. Then under each of the main headings list as many subpoints as you need to indicate the contents briefly. As in a summary, include all parts of the chapter in good proportion. An outline may look like this:

    I. Main Heading or Title of This Division (1:1-8)
       A. Subpoint (verses 1-3)
       B. Subpoint (4-8)
    II. Main Heading or Title of This Division (1:9-21)
       A. Subpoint (9-10)

   B. Subpoint (11-16)
    1. Sub-subpoint (11-13)
    2. Sub-subpoint (14-16)
   C. Subpoint (17-21)
  III. Main Heading or Title of This Division (1:22-25)

As an alternative, you may want to combine a summary and outline. To do this, find the main divisions of the chapter and title them as in an outline, indicating which verses are found in each division. Then summarize the contents of each division in a brief paragraph under the main heading.

Book Survey and Book Summary

As an option for a more thorough study, it is helpful to do a book survey during the first week of your study and a book summary the last week, after you have gone through the book chapter by chapter.

Book Survey—Here are seven steps to follow in your book survey:

1. Read the book through one to three times (at one sitting for each reading, if possible).

2. Make a tentative outline of the book to see its structure. The book may divide obviously into sections which you would identify with a heading pertaining to the content. A study Bible or a Bible handbook may help you form your tentative outline of the book.

3. Summarize the historical background of the book. For this you might use a reliable Bible dictionary or encyclopedia, a Bible handbook, or a study Bible. Jot down who wrote the book and to whom it was written. Write down when and where it was written and for what purpose.

4. List the major themes and highlights of the book. Try to discover these on your own before consulting a reference book. But if you have difficulty deciding on the major themes and highlights look for them in the outside helps.

5. List any key words you find in the book and any words that are repeated often.

6. Does the book have a key or summary verse? If so, make a note of it.

7. Read the book again (at one sitting, if possible), and write out a brief personal application on some portion of it.

Book Summary—Follow these nine steps for your book summary:

1. Review your book survey.

2. Reread the book one to three times. Read quickly and try to get the sweep of the whole book.

3. List your chapter titles and revise them if necessary.

4. Outline or summarize the entire book, using your chapter summaries or outlines as guides.

5. List your eminent truths by giving a one- or two-line summary of each one. List your basic verses. If one eminent truth for the whole book stands out, write a brief statement on it.

6. List your applications by using a short, descriptive title or a two-line summary for each.

7. Reread the book, referring to your chapter titles and your summary or outline (Items 3 and 4 above) as you read.

8. Write a title for the book. Try to make it identify the contents of the book.

9. List the main lessons and challenges you received from the book.

Summary

Again, your Advanced ABC Bible Study should include the following headings:

> TITLE
> APPLICATION
> BASIC PASSAGE
> CROSS-REFERENCES
> DIFFICULTIES
> EMINENT TRUTH
> FINAL STUDY (summary or outline)

Your study may also include a book survey and a book summary.

Enjoy your Advanced ABC Bible Study. As you continue in this method of chapter analysis, you will be building your personal Bible study library which will be an invaluable reference, both for your own review and as you help others.

If possible, find others to do the study with you. A group of from two to eight persons doing the same study and meeting together to share and discuss their discoveries can be greatly enriching.

BOOK: Philippians STUDY PASSAGE: Chapter 1

READ SLOWLY: Two times

READ ALOUD: Three times

VERSE BY VERSE MEDITATION: Once

OTHER TIMES READ: Twenty times

TIME SPENT ON THE STUDY: Five hours

TITLE: Positive Paul In Prison

APPLICATION:

Considering Paul's optimistic attitude — especially despite his circumstances — I too need to look for the positive more than I have been.

Paul continually focused on his power source — Christ. So I know that the only way I am going to be able to see the good in tough situations is to keep my focus on the Lord.

I will work at being more optimistic in my attitude and in my talking with others. It's a privilege to be doing the Lord's ministry, and I should find my optimism in Him and His promises, and not in present circumstances.

(AN EXAMPLE OF THE ADVANCED ABC BIBLE STUDY)

BASIC PASSAGE:

Philippians 1:21 "For me to live is Christ, and to die is gain."

CROSS-REFERENCES:

Vs.	Reference	Key Thought
1	Acts 16:1	Paul identified Timothy as being with him.
3	Colossians 1:3	Paul appreciated and prayed for the people he had ministered to in the past.
5	Acts 16:12-40	Paul recalled his memorable first visit to the Philippians. He was their partner in the Gospel.
6	II Cor. 1:14	When Christ returns, we can all rejoice because of our salvation.
11	John 15:5	As we are tied in to our source of strength, God will enable us to bring forth spiritual fruit.
21	Gal. 2:20	To live for Christ is to live by faith in Christ.
23	II Cor. 5:8	We must be willing and ready to be with God, separated from our bodies.
27	Ephesians 4:1	God has called all believers to a worthy job with responsibilities. We should live lives consistent with this calling.
29-30	Acts 16:19-24	Paul's conflict and suffering were real.

DIFFICULTIES:

Vs.	Question
11	What are the "fruits of righteousness"?

(AN EXAMPLE OF THE ADVANCED ABC BIBLE STUDY)

15,17	What does it mean that "Some indeed preach Christ from envy and rivalry" and "out of partisanship"?
20	How is Christ honored in my body by death?
22	How much of a choice do we have in living or dying?
27	How do I gauge whether my life is worthy of the Gospel of Christ?
29	Has suffering also been granted to me?

EMINENT TRUTH:

Involvement with people for the cause of Christ will bring both times of great joy and times of great trials. But in Christ, throughout everything, I can maintain a rejoicing attitude by concentrating on Him.

FINAL STUDY:
POSITIVE PAUL IN PRISON
(Philippians 1)

I. Paul's greeting (verses 1-11)
  A. In the name of the Lord (1-2)
  B. Thanksgiving and prayer for the Philippians (3-6)
  C. Reminder of his prayers and labor of love for them (7-8)
  D. Specific prayer for them (9-11)

II. Paul's account of prison (12-14)
  A. For the furtherance of the Gospel (12)
  B. The soldiers speak of Christ (13)
  C. Giving boldness to other believers (14)

III. Conflicting reasons for preaching the Gospel (15-17)

IV. Paul's attitude in prison (18-26)
  A. Rejoicing in the proclamation of Christ (18)
  B. Joyfully anticipating deliverance (19)
  C. Life or death (20-26)
    1. Christ honored in both (20)
    2. To die is gain (21)
    3. To live is to labor (22)
    4. He saw that believers at Philippi needed help (24)
    5. He resolved to be with them to help them (25-26)

(AN EXAMPLE OF THE ADVANCED ABC BIBLE STUDY)

I. Paul's exhortation from prison (27-30)
   A. For the Philippians to live exemplary lives as
      representatives of Jesus Christ (27)
   B. Not to be fearful of men (28)
   C. Expect suffering (29)
   D. Paul's life was the example (30)

CHAPTER TEN

HOW TO DO COMPREHENSIVE BOOK ANALYSIS

BUILDING still further on the Bible study methods described in previous chapters, Comprehensive Book Analysis includes a more thorough examination of the various aspects of the book you are studying. Another distinctive of this Bible study plan is that the book survey and the book summary are integral parts of the complete study, helping you see the book as a whole.

The books of the Bible were originally written as single units. For the sake of convenience, chapter and verse divisions were added many centuries later. For those who want to master the Bible, understanding the whole of each book leads to far better understanding of the particulars. And understanding the meaning of the particulars leads to proper conclusions and greater mastery of the Word of God. The Comprehensive Book Analysis Bible study plan enables the student to move from the *whole* to the *particulars* to a *conclusion*.

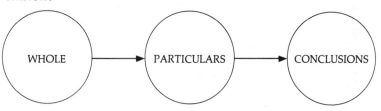

Three steps to studying any book of the Bible, then, are the book survey (the whole), chapter analysis (the particulars), and the book summary (conclusions).

In the study of each chapter, there are also three steps following the above procedure: the passage description (the whole), the verse-by-verse meditation (the particulars), and the theme and conclusion (conclusions). The whole study may be illustrated like this:

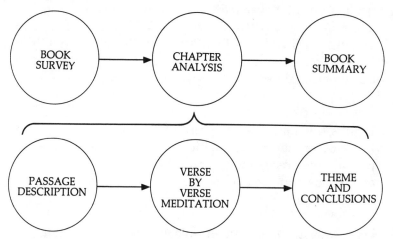

Since application may come from any step of the Bible study, it is not listed in the sequence above. The order illustrated represents the steps used to discern truth from God's Word. Application involves putting this truth into practice in daily life.

Getting Started

Begin your study by reviewing Unit One in this handbook, *The Basics of Bible Study*, then choose a New Testament book for your study. Eventually you may want to try an Old Testament book such as Jonah, Nehemiah, or Ruth.

A good pace is a chapter a week. If a chapter is particularly long, however, you may decide to do it in two studies. In addition, you should spend a week on the book survey as your first session and another week on the book summary as your last session. (For example, a six-chapter book like Ephesians would take eight weeks for your study.)

It is best to do your study in rough draft form first. Then organize your findings into final form.

HOW TO DO THE BOOK SURVEY

A book survey gives you an overview of the entire book. This overview will help you understand and relate the particulars you discover later. The book survey contains five main sections: PRINCIPAL PERSONALITIES, HISTORICAL SETTING, PURPOSE, THEMES, and OVERVIEW. You may also want to list the style, key words, additional personalities, and the geography of the book.

Principal Personalities

Who is the author of the book? To whom was he writing? What other major personalities are mentioned in the book? How do they relate to one another? How well do they know and understand one another?

Historical Setting

When was the book written? What is the historical setting in which it was written? What is the historical background of the recipients? What was happening in that part of the world at that time?

Purpose

Why was this book written? If there was a problem to correct, what was it? What was the writer trying to accomplish?

Themes

What is the major emphasis of the book? What are some of the recurring ideas? What subjects does the author deal with?

Overview

Summarize the book in an outline, chart, or diagram form. You may want to use the theme and outline given in a reference book for a starting point. As you complete your study you will write your own theme and outline.

Other Observations

Other questions which may be important include:

1. What is the style of writing? Does the author use such elements as illustrations, logical arguments, and emotional appeals?

2. What are the key words in the book?

3. What is the lifestyle of the personalities? What is their culture like? What are some of their customs and habits?

4. How does the geography and topography of the places mentioned help you understand the book?

Many other possibilities exist to make your study more interesting. Some of these questions become more important in studying particular books. The more you study, the more you will be able to discern which questions are important to ask.

Most of this information can be found in a variety of sources. You can find background material for a book survey in the following reference books:

1. A reliable Bible dictionary or encyclopedia.

2. A good, contemporary Bible handbook.

3. An up-to-date Bible atlas.

4. A trustworthy Bible survey.

5. A simple, English-text commentary.

6. An exhaustive concordance or word study book.

Don't be afraid to use reference materials. These books usually reflect years of study done by men of God. On the other hand, do not rely on them completely, for they are not infallible.

HOW TO DO THE CHAPTER ANALYSIS

When working on your chapter analysis, you will begin with a passage description, then do a verse-by-verse meditation, and finish with your theme and conclusions. These will all contribute toward your application.

The chapter analysis Bible study incorporates the Bible study essentials of *observation*, *interpretation*, and *application*. In the passage description, you will make observations on the passage as a whole; in the verse-by-verse meditation, you will make observations on each verse, ask questions to help you interpret the verse, and use cross-references to correlate the verse with the rest of the Bible. You will draw these thoughts together and record them in the theme and conclusion section. Finally, you will write out your application in the application section.

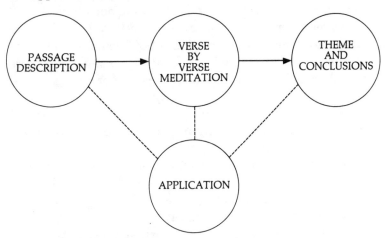

The Passage Description

Read through the passage several times and briefly describe the overall contents. While you may want to supplement your reading from one of the more recent Bible translations or paraphrases, be sure to use a standard version for your basic study.

Do not attempt to analyze or interpret when writing your passage description. Carefully observe what is being said, not why. After reading your passage description, another person familiar with the passage should be able to identify it. While there are many ways to describe a passage, the basic content of the passage should be uniform. Remember to use the principles of observation (pages 20-21), and do not overlook the obvious in your description.

One method of describing a passage is to rewrite it without the modifying phrases and clauses. This basically leaves the subjects, verbs, and objects. It is especially effective when the passage contains many modifiers. You can readily observe the movement of the passage by rewriting it in this manner.

Another method of describing a passage is to make a summary outline. The first step is to divide the passage into paragraphs. Most of the recent versions of the Bible already have suggested paragraph breaks. The original text was not divided into paragraphs, so you may want to divide your passage differently. Noticing changes of subject and natural divisions will help you determine the possible paragraph divisions. After determining your paragraph divisions, write a sentence or two summarizing each paragraph's contents. Don't be concerned if you omit some details, but give a general framework which you can fit the details into later.

Verse-by-verse Meditation

The verse-by-verse meditation gives you an opportunity to make further observations and interpret and correlate the passage. At this point in the study you will take a prolonged look at the details as you proceed from one verse to the next. The Bible study essentials of observation, interpretation, and application are used here to study each individual *verse* as well as the entire passage.

Place your findings under three headings in this section: OBSERVATIONS, QUESTIONS AND ANSWERS, and CROSS-REFERENCES. These are three important aspects of verse-by-verse meditation. Place the verse numbers on the left of your findings under each heading. The fourth heading in this section is NOTES AND COMMENTS.

The objective is to meditate on the verse, not to write something about every verse in every column. Take a concentrated look at each verse, noting on paper your observations, questions, answers, and cross-references. Record additional information and possible applications under NOTES AND COMMENTS. Use extra sheets of paper if necessary to record all your findings.

Observations—Proper observation is the foundation on which good interpretation and application are built. Since it is impossible to record every observation, record the observations which stimulate you to further thinking. You will also want to record observations on the relationship of the specific verse to other verses in the same passage.

Questions—This section takes considerable time and effort, but it often leads to rewarding meditations. As you grow in your knowledge of the Bible, you will have more questions, and they will be increasingly penetrating and significant. At the same time, your own knowledge and understanding will increase. There is no limit to the number or variety of questions for any particular passage.

Answers—When a question has several possible answers, you may record more than one. The Scriptures do not always provide clearcut answers for every issue, so be careful not to insist on always finding one. Major on what God has revealed plainly. Sometimes it is best to write questions without trying to answer them. This allows you time to think about them. Waiting may keep you from pursuing unnecessary tangents, and in some cases a succeeding verse will answer your question.

In many cases, a question will stimulate further study in other sources. But you will want to find most answers from the Bible itself. Often a cross-reference will help.

Cross-references—The Bible is its own best commentary. Scripture interprets Scripture. The content of one passage clarifies the content of another. To help you apply this principle, use both internal and external cross-references. An internal cross-reference is located in the same book as the verse being studied; an external cross-reference comes from another portion of Scripture.

Internal cross-references show the relationship of a verse to the paragraph, the chapter, and the book in which it is found. This helps place the verse in its context. Whenever a verse uses a connective word such as *wherefore, and, therefore,* or *hence*, an internal cross-reference will show what it refers to. External cross-references show how the verse being studied relates to verses in other books in the Bible. It is especially noteworthy to find other writers of Scripture who have said essentially the same thing. Important types of external cross-references are parallel (saying the same thing), corresponding (dealing with similar matter), contrasting, and illustrative.

The best source of cross-references is your own memory and knowledge of the Bible. If you cannot find one on your own, use a concordance or the marginal notes in your Bible. If you are looking for a verse which contains a key word, don't hesitate to use a concordance, but don't fall into the trap of relying on it completely rather than thinking for yourself. (*The Treasury of Scripture Knowledge*, published by Fleming H. Revell Company, is a book which lists 500,000 cross-references from all books of the Bible.)

In the space next to the cross-reference add your linking thought—the thought that relates this cross-reference to the verse being studied. Use a short phrase or key words from the reference to help you retain its content.

Notes and Comments—Use the space under this heading for your own study emphasis. You may want to title it with a specific topic or to list such things as implications, possible applications, illustrations, definitions, and additional observations.

The Theme and Conclusions

By the time you come to the THEME and CONCLUSIONS sections of your chapter analysis, you will have done a considerable amount of study. You will have described the passage, meditated on each verse, made observations, asked questions, discovered answers, and found cross-references.

The theme is the central issue discussed by the writer of the book you are studying. It may be a topic, a proposition, a problem, or an argument. You may find more than one theme in a particular passage.

The best way to arrive at the theme is to ask yourself for each paragraph, "What is the author talking about?" or, "What is the basic subject of this paragraph?" Combining and summarizing the paragraph themes will help you determine the major theme of the passage.

After arriving at the theme or themes of the passage, begin to record the conclusions. In each paragraph there may be more than one conclusion because the author may be saying more than one thing about the subject. The most accurate way to arrive at conclusions is to ask, "What is the author saying about the theme?" or "What is being said about the topic or subject of each paragraph?" It is not as important to have a great number of conclusions as it is to have conclusions which follow logically from the main themes running through the passage.

You will also want to title the chapter. Your title will probably reflect the theme and conclusions you discovered earlier.

The Application

Bible study without application leads to vain knowledge. Dwight L. Moody said, "The Scriptures were not given to increase our knowledge, but to change our lives."

Recording your application will help you clarify what you plan to do. It also encourages you to be specific. It is easy to say, "I am going to pray more." That type of application is seldom put into practice. It is far more meaningful to write down, "I am going to spend the first five minutes of my lunch break each day in prayer."

The following four questions may help you write meaningful applications:

1. What is the truth I want to apply?
2. What is my need?

3. What is my plan of action?

4. How can I check my progress?

Pray for the Holy Spirit's help in selecting and carrying out your application.

HOW TO DO THE BOOK SUMMARY

To complete your study of a book of the Bible you will need to tie together what you have learned in a book summary. Your book summary will help you unify knowledge, consolidate facts, and grasp the whole book.

The first step in the summary is to reread the book several times. Do each reading at one sitting if possible. Since the material is now familiar, you should be able to read it rapidly. Look for the general thread that runs through the book. Try to get an overall view.

Review your chapter titles to help you determine the general flow, and write an outline for the whole book. You will find it interesting to compare your final outline with the overview in your book survey.

Next, review your passage themes and main conclusions. Decide which theme or themes are most important and list them. Now do the same thing with your conclusions, choosing the most crucial ones.

Consider the book as a whole and give it a title. Try to keep your title short and use words that are picturesque or illustrative of the book's contents.

Finally, review your applications for each passage. Are there any applications you haven't completed? From your review, write out your final application and make definite plans to complete it.

* * *

Summary

The major headings in your book survey should be:
PRINCIPAL PERSONALITIES
HISTORICAL SETTING

PURPOSE
THEMES
OVERVIEW

In your chapter analysis, the headings should be:

PASSAGE DESCRIPTION
OBSERVATIONS
QUESTIONS AND ANSWERS
CROSS-REFERENCES
NOTES AND COMMENTS
TITLE
THEME
CONCLUSIONS
APPLICATION

The headings in your book summary should be:

BOOK TITLE
FINAL OUTLINE
MAIN THEME
MAIN CONCLUSIONS
FINAL APPLICATION

SURVEY

BOOK: 1 Thessalonians

PRINCIPAL PERSONALITIES:

Paul, the author; Timothy and Silas (Silvanus) co-workers with Paul while he ministered to the Thessalonians

HISTORICAL SETTING:

Paul, Silas, and Timothy went about 100 miles south west of Philippi to Thessalonica (Acts 17). They spent about three weeks there and a growing church was begun. Paul probably wrote this letter after his visit while in Athens (A.D. 52) This is the earliest of Paul's epistles.

PURPOSE:

To overcome problems with Paul's character and ministry, to instruct on the doctrine of the return of Christ and to encourage them while they were being persecuted.

THEMES:

The Second Coming of Christ
Paul's Personal Ministry
Purity of Life

STYLE: Personal, reminiscent, instructional

KEY WORDS: God the Father, Jesus Christ, Holy Spirit, Faith, Love, Hope, Joy

GEOGRAPHY: Thessalonica was the capital of Macedonia on the commercial trade route. It became a free city after the battle of Philippi (42 B.C.).

(AN EXAMPLE OF COMPREHENSIVE BOOK ANALYSIS)

OVERVIEW:

I. Personal—Paul's past and present dealings with the Thessalonian church (Chapters 1-3)

A. Greeting (1:1)

B. Thanksgiving (1:2-10)

C. The ministry of the apostles (2:1-20)

  1. As evangelists (2:1-6)

  2. As pastors (2:7-9)

  3. As teachers (2:10-12)

  4. The result of the apostles' ministry (2:13-16)

  5. Satanic opposition to the ministry (2:17-18)

  6. The reward of the ministry (2:19-20)

D. Progress of the church (3:1-13)

  1. Timothy sent to Thessalonica (3:1-5)

  2. Timothy brings back good tidings (3:6-13)

II. Practical—Instruction concerning the life Christians should live in view of the immediate return of the Lord (Chapters 4-5)

A. Instruction in holiness (4:1-8)

B. Instruction regarding love of brethren (4:9-10)

C. Instruction regarding conduct toward those outside the church (4:11-12)

D. Instruction regarding rapture of the saints (4:13-1

E. Instruction regarding the revelation of Christ (5:1-11

F. Various instructions (5:12-28)

(From The Bible Book by Book by G. Coleman Luck, Moody Press)

(AN EXAMPLE OF COMPREHENSIVE BOOK ANALYSIS)

CHAPTER ANALYSIS

PASSAGE: 1 Thessalonians 1

PASSAGE DESCRIPTION:

vs. 1-5

After a word of greeting, Paul tells how thankful he is for the quality of life in the Thessalonian church.

vs. 6-10

In following Paul's example, the Thessalonians became a growing influence throughout Macedonia and Achaia. Every where people spoke about their response to God.

TITLE:

The Gospel and Paul's Effective Ministry in Thessalonica

THEME:

Paul's Gospel in Thessalonica (vs.1-5)
Paul's Effective Ministry in Thessalonica (vs.6-10)

(AN EXAMPLE OF COMPREHENSIVE BOOK ANALYSIS)

VS. OBSERVATION	VS. QUESTIONS AND ANSWERS
1 A letter from three men who probably traveled together	1 When were they in Thessalonica?
2 Paul gives thanks for them (denotes his personal concern)	2 What did Paul pray for them (Eph. 1:17-21; 3:16-21)
3 Three parallel thoughts: 1. work of faith 2. labor of love 3. steadfastness of hope	3 What is faith? Trusting in God's character + obeying Him. What is steadfastness of hope? "Patient waiting for Christ, enduring trials until He comes."
4 God chose me!	4 When did God choose me?
5 Gospel can be communicated in: a. power b. the Holy Spirit c. full conviction	5 What is conviction? "Describes the willingness of freedom of spirit enjoyed by those who brought the Gospel to Thess."
6 They were imitators of Paul	6 Whom are we to imitate?
8 "Word" mentioned also vs 5,6 Faith is directed toward God Faith always has an object	8 Where is Macedonia? Achaia? North of Greece, M. was conquered by Rome in 168 B.C.
9 Ministry had 3 effects: 1. turned to God from idols 2. serving a living God 3. wait for Son from heaven	9 Was idol worship a common practice?
10 Christ's resurrection is linked with His coming again	10 Is resurrection commonly linked with Second Coming?

(AN EXAMPLE OF COMPREHENSIVE BOOK ANALYSIS)

VS. CROSS-REFERENCES	NOTES AND COMMENTS
1-Acts 17:1 After they visited Amphipolis + Apollonia	Maybe I should write Joe a follow-up letter
2-I Thess. 5:18 Give thanks in everything	Do a topical study on thanksgiving
3-II Thess. 3:5 Steadfastness of Christ Heb. 11:1 Faith is confident assurance of the unseen and future	Am I enduring under trials? Am I focusing on Christ as my hope?
4-II Thess. 2:13 From the beginning 5-Col. 2:2 Full assurance or conviction of understanding results in knowing Christ	Do I really know how to explain the Gospel? Need to work on memorizing a simple plan of salvation.
6-I Cor. 11:1 Follow me as I follow Christ	How can I be a better example?
8-Acts 16:9 Paul had a vision to go to Macedonia	What is my faith directed toward?
9-Acts 19:19 Ephesians burned their idols and magic books	Am I worshipping any idols?
10-I Thess. 4:16,17 Links resurrection with Second Coming	

(AN EXAMPLE OF COMPREHENSIVE BOOK ANALYSIS)

CONCLUSIONS:

Prayer, preaching, and the demonstration of power are three keys to communicating the Gospel (vs. 2,5)

An effective Gospel ministry includes being imitators to some and examples to others (vs. 6, 7)

Turning to God from idols is a work of faith, serving a living God is a labor of love and waiting for His Son is steadfastness of hope (vs. 3, 9, 10).

APPLICATION:

The truth of 1 Thess. 1:9 is to turn from idols and focus on Christ.

My need results from making money my idol. I hold on too tightly to my paycheck and possessions and am selfish with how I spend what God has given.

I will plan to draw up a budget this week and give at least 10% to Christ's work. I will also memorize 1 Thess. 1:9, 10

I will check myself by sharing my application with my roommate and having him review my verses with me.

SUMMARY

BOOK: 1 Thessalonians

BOOK TITLE: "A Way of Life for New Christians"

FINAL OUTLINE:

I. The Effects of the Gospel on the Thessalonians (1:1-10).

II. Paul's Personal Ministry to the Thessalonians (2:1-20).

III. God's Purpose for the Lives of the Thessalonians (3:1-4:12).

IV. Expectation for the Return of Christ (4:13-18)

V. A Challenge to a Changed Life for the Thessalonians (5:1-28).

MAIN THEMES:

The hope of Christ's return inspires (1:8-10), rewards (2:17-20), purifies (4:1-12), comforts (4:13-18) and awakens to action (5:1-10).

Faith produces work (1:3,9) love produces labor (1:3,9) and hope produces patience (1:3,10).

The purpose of afflictions is to produce sanctification in the believer (1:6; 2:14-16; 3:7-10; 5:1-10).

(AN EXAMPLE OF COMPREHENSIVE BOOK ANALYSIS)

MAIN CONCLUSIONS:

The hope of Christ's return permeates a Christian's beliefs.
Faith, hope, and love are to be the model attitudes and
sparks to action.
Afflictions are not to be feared, but enjoyed as sources
of growth and development.

FINAL APPLICATION:

I want to memorize verses in 1 Thessalonians
that relate to encouraging others with hope (2:19, 20;
3:11-13; 4:15-18; 5:9, 11) and to begin to share these
truths with others, beginning with my roommate who's a
new Christian.

CHAPTER ELEVEN

HOW TO DO
A TOPICAL BIBLE STUDY

MUCH of our personal Bible study is aimed at finding what God wants us to do, as well as what He wants us to know. These two emphases are right, for one without the other would get us out of balance. Paul's statement that "all Scripture is God-breathed and is useful for teaching, rebuking, correcting and training in righteousness" (2 Timothy 3:16) includes both knowing and doing, but emphasizes doing:

- *teaching*—what we should know;
- *rebuking*—what we should avoid doing;
- *correcting*—what we should do differently;
- *training in righteousness*—what we should begin or continue doing.

One good way to help you discover God's will is through studying a *topic* in Scripture. In a topical study you will try to draw together and summarize what the Bible says on a given subject.

This study is for your own personal use and reference and should not aim at being exhaustive or scholarly. It should serve to reveal the key truths of Scripture about your topic and point out what you need to know and do about it—to change your life and to help you teach others.

Choose a Good Topic

Your topic for study may be one you have long wanted to research. It may have come up as a side issue during a chapter analysis or other type of study. Or perhaps you heard a sermon that started you thinking on this subject. You may be discipling someone who has asked you searching questions on a matter of importance to him, and you need some answers. So this is your opportunity to study a topic of current interest to you directly from the Scriptures. You can come out with your own personalized set of conclusions—and even convictions—on the subject, complete with application to your own needs.

If you select a topic that is quite broad, such as *Love*, you could divide it into several studies, such as *The Love of God, Man's Love for God, Love of Neighbor*, or *The Nature of Love*.

Here is a random listing of topics.

Anger	Marriage
Citizenship	Obedience
Courage	Parent/Child
Discipleship	Relationships
Evangelism	Patience
Faith	Prayer
Fear	Priorities
Follow-up	Purity
Fruitfulness	The Quiet Time
Giving	Salvation
Godliness	Scripture Memory
God's Guidance	Self-discipline
The Gospel	Sin
Grace	Steadfastness
Holiness	Thankfulness
The Holy Spirit	Wealth and Possessions
Humility	Witnessing
Integrity	The Word of God
The Lordship of Christ	World Vision
Love	Worship

Getting Started

Review Unit One in this handbook, *The Basics of Bible Study*, and follow these directions:

Select Scripture Passages

Once you have selected your topic, you are ready to select the 10 to 12 *best* passages on the topic. Use scratch paper as you jot down possible portions of Scripture and decide which are the best. It is best to do your study in rough draft form first and organize it later in final form.

A concordance will help you find passages relating to your topic. Look up closely related words as well as the main one. (If your topic is *Salvation*, for example, look up such words as *forgiveness*, *redemption*, *born again*, *atonement*, and *eternal life*.)

You might also use the *New Topical Text Book* (Revell), *Harper's Topical Concordance* (Harper & Row), or *Nave's Topical Bible* (Moody) to find the passages you want to select. Or you could skim through parts of the Bible and jot down the references of those portions where your topic is treated. If your Bible has a subject index, you might find some references on your topic listed there.

Some passages you will select will be a single verse, others a paragraph or maybe a whole chapter.

This process of selecting the best passages will take some time as you look up and compare various Scriptures. But don't become frustrated trying to choose them. Be patient; once you have chosen your dozen or so best passages, you will have put some limits around your study and you won't wander endlessly through the Bible searching for one more tidbit of truth.

Of course, *all* Scripture is inspired and profitable. But in this part of your study you are simply trying to choose the important passages which best relate to your study and add certain facts or illustrations not represented by the other passages you have chosen. List the 10 to 12 references with a key thought beside each one for quick identification.

Summarize or Outline

The Scriptures you have chosen and listed form the basis for the rest of your topical study. It may help to consider this list of Scriptures as you would a single chapter in a chapter analysis study.

Summarize separately the content of each passage. Then read through the summaries one or more times, noting the main points the passages teach and how they fit together. On another sheet of paper write a summary of your summaries, condensing, rearranging, and combining where possible. This should be a composite statement of what the Scripture teaches on your topic. Or you may prefer to state the truths you have discovered in outline form, once you have written your summaries. When you have rewritten the summary or outline to your satisfaction, copy it in final form on a separate sheet of paper or your study blank.

Find the Key Verse

As you read through each of the Scripture passages for study, find one that seems to contain the kernel of what the Bible teaches on this topic. Or if you prefer, simply choose the verse you like best on the topic. Record it under the heading KEY VERSE or FAVORITE VERSE. You may want to memorize this verse as a reminder of the topic.

Collect Illustrations

Your Scripture passages for study, as well as your summary or outline, may contain some illustrations of the topic. If so, list them by reference under the heading ILLUSTRATIONS. For example, in a study on *Faith* you might use Abraham as an illustration, listing Hebrews 11:8-10.

You may also think of other illustrations from the Bible, from your own life, from nature, or from the experiences of others that you could add here. Clippings and poems that illustrate the subject may also be enclosed. This section of the study will be especially helpful if you are called on to teach or speak on the subject.

Record Problems

Read again through the Scripture passages, and find and write down things that puzzle you, or things you think might be hard for some other Christians to understand. Under the heading PROBLEMS, list the reference for the verse which presented the problem, and write a question that describes the problem.

For example, for the topic *Humility* a problem might be listed for James 4:10 as, "How is it possible to humble *ourselves*?"

Write an Application

Review the other parts of your study and go back over each of the Scripture passages, asking God to show you some aspect of the truth that you should apply in your life.

First, write a brief statement of the truth contained in the verse or verses you select for your application. Then add a brief statement of the need or condition in your life, in your relationship to the Lord or in your relationship to others, which should be changed or improved according to the truth you have learned or about which you have been reminded.

Finally, record a simple plan of action you will follow to help bring about the needed correction or build the quality into your life. This might be spending time in prayer about the need, memorizing a verse of Scripture, making restitution to someone, doing some kindness, or scheduling a special project. A vast number of possibilities exist for carrying out applications you make. This is the cream of your study and should always be exciting—though not always easy—as you see God work in your life according to His promise.

Summary

Your Topical Bible Study should include the following headings:

> TOPIC
> SCRIPTURE PASSAGES STUDIED
> SUMMARY or OUTLINE

KEY VERSE or FAVORITE VERSE
ILLUSTRATIONS
PROBLEMS
APPLICATION

As with other Navigator studies, the Topical Bible Study can be most rewarding when worked out individually and later discussed in a group. Groups of two to eight persons are best; more than eight could become unwieldy. Your own discoveries will be refreshing and helpful to others, as well as theirs to you.

TOPIC: The Prayers of Jesus

PASSAGES STUDIED:

Reference	Identifying Thought
Hebrews 5:7	He prayed with the strongest emotion and effort to His Father.
Matthew 26:27	At the Last Supper, He gave thanks for the bread.
Matthew 27:46	On the Cross, He cried out in yearning for God.
Luke 5:15-16	Sometimes when the crowd grew, He went away to pray alone.
Luke 6:12	He spent the entire night in prayer on the mountain.
Luke 10:21	He praised God, rejoicing greatly in the Holy Spirit.
Luke 22:31-32	He prayed for Simon Peter, that his faith would not fail.
Luke 22:39-44	In agony, and very fervently, He prayed in Gethsemane for God's will to be done.
Luke 23:34	He prayed for forgiveness for those who crucified Him.
Luke 23:46	Just before dying, He committed His soul to God.
John 11:41-43	Before calling Lazarus out from the tomb, He gave thanks.
John 17	For His followers, He prayed for God's protection, their joy, their sanctification, their unity, and their presence in glory with Him.

(AN EXAMPLE OF A TOPICAL BIBLE STUDY)

SUMMARY:

Jesus, God's only Son, perfect and holy, has demonstrated for all time how the Christian should pray. He prayed continually — for as long as an entire night, but also in momentary sentences of praise and thanksgiving. He prayed with extreme emotion, seeking God's will and God's glory. He prayed for His closest followers, for the entire Church — and for His enemies.

"To pray in the name of Christ is to pray as Christ Himself prayed" — J.G.Thomson.

FAVORITE VERSE: Hebrews 5:7 — "In the days of His flesh . . . He offered up both prayers and supplications with loud crying and tears to Him who was able to save Him from death, and . . . was heard because of His piety."

(AN EXAMPLE OF A TOPICAL BIBLE STUDY)

ILLUSTRATIONS:

"The fountain-head from which all [the New Testament's] instruction in prayer flows is Christ's own doctrine and practice"—J. G. Thomson, The New Bible Dictionary, p.1021.

PROBLEMS:

Reference	Identifying Question
Matthew 27:46	How had God forsaken Christ?
Luke 23:24	Were His crucifiers any less guilty for not understanding fully what they were doing?

APPLICATION:

I will spend at least an hour in prayer before dawn tomorrow, reviewing these passages as I pray, and praising God.

(AN EXAMPLE OF A TOPICAL BIBLE STUDY)

CHAPTER TWELVE

HOW TO DO A BIBLE CHARACTER STUDY

THE Bible is alive with personality. It includes numerous accounts of the lives of individuals, and we can read about their relationships both to God and to one another. This inspired and infallible record has been preserved for us through the centuries, and is still a great source of teaching for us today. The Apostle Paul wrote, "Everything that was written in the past was written to teach us, so that through endurance and the encouragement of the Scriptures we might have hope" (Romans 15:4).

These Bible characters were real everyday humans like us. Even Elijah, one of the greatest men of all time, is described in this way: "Elijah was a man just like us" (James 5:17). It was his life lived in obedience to God that made him great.

There is much to learn by studying how the lives of these individuals were touched by God, how they responded to God, what kinds of persons they became, and what mark they left on their times.

Getting Started

Review Unit One in this handbook, *The Basics of Bible Study*, and follow these directions:

Scriptures Used

Once you have selected the subject for your Bible Character Study, list the character's name (and any limitations on your study of that character) under the heading PERSON STUDIED. Then choose and list the passages of Scripture you will use for your study. A good Bible dictionary or encyclopedia or an exhaustive concordance will tell you where the person is mentioned. The index in a study Bible may also help. It is best to do your study in rough draft form first, and later to neatly organize it into final form.

Some people in the Bible have little written about them, and you will want to include every reference to them in your study. Others, such as David, have so much written about them that you will have to select the passages you think are most significant. Use scratch paper as you look up various references; eliminate some and keep the others. When you have decided on the passages you will use, list them, and add a key thought for quick identification of each reference.

Biographical Sketch

Read each of your selected Scripture passages several times and meditate on them. Then begin writing a brief biography of the person. This will be mainly the facts of the character's life, without interpretation. Include such things as the meaning of his name, when and where he lived, and his family background. Record any unusual influences or environmental factors which shaped his life and thinking, as well as his occupation and his contemporaries and associates. What were the major events in his life? Mention the growth of his relationship with God, his crowning achievement and contribution, his influence on his nation and family, and anything else of interest about him.

When you have included everything you think belongs in his biographical sketch, rewrite it, condensing and rearranging parts as needed to make a one- to three-paragraph summary of his life.

Key Verse

Choose from your list of Scriptures a key verse for your subject's life. This will be a verse, or pair of verses, which more than any other sums up his life.

If you cannot find such a verse, then choose one which speaks of his outstanding characteristic. For example, a key verse *summarizing* Noah's life might be Hebrews 11:7, while one *characterizing* the life of Mary of Bethany could be John 12:3.

NOTE: A *summary* verse will probably come from your Scriptures chosen for study, while you may want to look elsewhere for a *characteristic* verse (Psalms or Proverbs, for example).

The key verse from your study might well be one you will want to memorize.

Leading Lesson

Read through your Scriptures and your biographical sketch again. What do you see as the leading lesson of this person's life?

Perhaps your key verse holds a clue to the leading lesson. It might be positive or negative, something worthy of following or something that should be avoided. The leading lessons in the lives of two women mentioned in the genealogy of Jesus Christ, for instance, might be *the reward of faith* for Rahab and *the deceitfulness of idols* in the case of Rachel.

When you have decided on the leading lesson for your subject, write it down and give a little background of the passage from which you chose it. Then tell why you think this is the leading lesson to be learned from this person's life.

Problems

As you study, some things may cross your mind that are problems to you—either about your subject or about God's dealings with him. List these things under the heading PROBLEMS. Don't try to resolve them now; just write down the nature of your questions. Later you can track down some answers, or perhaps discover that God has not made the answers available to us.

Application

Review the other parts of your study and go back over the Scripture passages. Ask the Lord to show you some principle you should apply or some characteristic you need to build or strengthen—or avoid—in your life.

Write under the heading APPLICATION the principle or characteristic you have decided on through prayer, and include the Scripture passage from which it is taken.

Add a sentence or two about what needs to be corrected or improved in your life along the lines of this principle or characteristic. If you can refer to a specific example of the attitudes or actions you need to change, this will clarify your application and also help you see the changes in your life as you look back later.

Now record what you plan to do in cooperation with the Holy Spirit to help conform your life more into the image of Christ. Your part is to yield your will to Him and take steps to obey what He has shown you in His Word.

Your step of action might be to do more Bible study on certain subjects, spend a stated time in intercessory prayer, visit the sick, do something practical for the needy, or any number of things, according to the need you have recognized. If, for example, your need is for self-sacrificing care for others, you might plan to deprive yourself of funds, leisure time, or privileges in order to spend those resources on someone who cannot repay you. Ideas for carrying out your application will come as you seek them.

Summary

Your Bible Character Study should include these headings:
PERSON STUDIED
SCRIPTURES USED
BIOGRAPHICAL SKETCH

KEY VERSE
LEADING LESSON
PROBLEMS
APPLICATION

As with other Navigator Bible studies, the Bible Character Study can be most rewarding when worked out individually and later discussed in a group. Groups of two to eight persons are best; more than eight could become unwieldy. Jot down any good ideas from others' studies that you can use in the future and share yours with them.

PERSON STUDIED: Nehemiah

SCRIPTURES USED:

Vs.	Key Thought
Nehemiah 1:4	Intense feeling for the distress of his people
1:9	Claimed God's promise
2:5-9	Trusted God, yet planned in detail
2:20	Gave God credit for success
4:14	Taught fearful people to remember God and family
5:15	Set an unselfish example out of reverence for God
6:13	Enemies devised a plot to ruin his reputation
8:10	Encouraged the people to rejoice in God
13:14	Expressed desire for God's recognition
13:25	Harsh in dealing with sin among the people

BIOGRAPHICAL SKETCH:

Nehemiah, whose name means "comfort of God," lived during the reign of the Persian King Artaxerxes. The events recorded in the Book of Nehemiah occurred around 445 to 433 B.C. Nehemiah was a cupbearer to King Artaxerxes, a job which required him to test the king's food for poisoning (International Standard Bible Encyclopedia, p. 2131).

(AN EXAMPLE OF A BIBLE CHARACTER STUDY)

The city of Jerusalem had been destroyed to the point that the protective walls of the city needed reconstruction. Nehemiah was granted permission and all necessary provisions by Artaxerxes to rebuild the city. Under his direction, the wall was completed.

During the time that Nehemiah served as governor in Jerusalem, he also challenged the Jews on such issues as unjust business practices and marrying foreign wives.

KEY VERSE: Nehemiah 2:17

"Then I said to them, 'You see the bad situation we are in, that Jerusalem is desolate and its gates burned by fire. Come, let us rebuild the wall of Jerusalem that we may no longer be a reproach'" (NASB).

LEADING LESSON:

James 2:17 "Even so faith, if it has no works, is dead, being by itself" (NASB).

Nehemiah is an example of a man who demonstrated his faith by his works. He believed God could overcome all obstacles in the way of rebuilding Jerusalem, and was willing to step out and act in light of that belief.

PROBLEMS:

Vs.	Identifying Questions
Nehemiah 4:5	Jesus taught us to pray for our enemies, not against them. Nehemiah prayed against his enemies. Was this right?
Nehemiah 13:25	How often is such harshness needed in dealing with sin?

(AN EXAMPLE OF A BIBLE CHARACTER STUDY)

APPLICATION:

Nehemiah was a man of action. He saw a need and even though it was costly and dangerous he took the opportunity to help meet the need.

I felt as I read the account of his life that willingness and availability make the difference. Though Nehemiah was a cup bearer and not a construction foreman, he was available to help build the wall at Jerusalem.

As an application, I am going to evaluate my attitude and schedule in light of being available to needs. I realize I am not responsive to needs if they appear too big or difficult. But to trust God is to rely on His sufficiency and ability to overcome obstacles.

I now have some opportunities to help others, yet I haven't been very available. This week I will prayerfully evaluate my schedule and make whatever changes are necessary to be free to help.

The opportunities for helping which I will consider include:

1. Joining the evangelism program at church.
2. Spending more time with Harry and Jim.
3. More involvement with the people in my Sunday School class.

(AN EXAMPLE OF A BIBLE CHARACTER STUDY)

APPENDIX

A SUGGESTED LONG-RANGE
BIBLE STUDY PROGRAM

THIS suggested program is arranged for 45 weeks of study each year. For your studies of each book, a week is allowed for studying each chapter, and for an introductory survey study, and a concluding summary study. (This means that seven weeks are allowed for a five-chapter book such as 1 Thessalonians.) Topical and character studies are *italicized*. The order of topical studies assumes you are already fairly well grounded in basic doctrines through question-and-answer studies.

This program is not meant to be rigid; you may adjust it as you feel you need to for your own study program.

First Year	*Weeks*
1 Thessalonians	7
1 John	7
Philippians	6
Salvation	2
Witnessing	2
Follow-up	2
Gospel of Mark	18
Character: Daniel	1

Eighth Year	*Weeks*
3 John	1
Jude	1
Humility	1
Honesty	1
Revelation	24
Judgment and Hell	2
Character: Nehemiah	2
Genesis 1	1
Genesis 12	1
Philemon	1
Time Management	1
Character: Peter	5
Judges 7	1
1 Kings 18	1
Job 1	1
Job 2	1

Ninth Year	
Gospel of Matthew	30
Correction and Rebuke	1
2 Kings 17	1
Psalm 40	1
Numbers 14	1
Faithfulness—God's; Man's Required	2
Psalm 103	1
Deuteronomy 4	1
Joshua 3	1
Jonah (4 chapters)	6

Nine-year Summary:	
27 New Testament books (all)	306
30 *topical studies*	49
11 *character studies*	18
30 Old Testament chapters	32
Nine years at 45 weeks per year	405

In the tenth year you may begin again, selecting from the previous nine, or you may add any other Old Testament books, topics, and biographies that you desire.

VERSE ANALYSIS

Date: _____

Verse for study: _____

_____

_____

Message: (What does the verse say?) _____

_____

_____

_____

_____

_____

_____

_____

Context:

What thoughts do the preceding verses add? _____

_____

_____

_____

_____

What thoughts do the following verses add? _____

_____

_____

_____

Questions:

_____

_____

_____

_____

_____

_____

_____

_____

_____

_____

_____

_____

Application:_____

_____

_____

_____

_____

_____

_____

_____

_____

_____

_____

THE ABC BIBLE STUDY

te: _____

dy passage: _____

Title: _____

☐ Best verse or ☐ Basic passage:

_____

Challenge:

rse of the challenge: _____

uth of the challenge: _____

_____

_____

_____

_____

_____

_____

rsonal application of the challenge: _____

_____

_____

_____

_____

_____

_____

_____

_____

_____

_____

_____

D. Difficulties:

Verse:	Difficulty:

E. Essence: (summary or outline)

SEARCH THE SCRIPTURES

Date: _____

Study passage: _____

Point of the passage: (What does it say?)

_____

_____

_____

_____

_____

_____

_____

_____

_____

_____

_____

_____

_____

Parallel passages: (What does it say elsewhere in Scripture?)

Verse:	Reference:	Key thought:

Problems of the passage: (What does it say that I don't understand?)

Verse:	Question:

Profit of the passage: (What does it say to me?)

HE ADVANCED
C BIBLE STUDY

te: _____

dy passage: _____

es read:
  Slowly: _____   Aloud: _____   In verse-by-verse meditation: _____

  Other times: _____   Time spent on the study: _____

e: _____

plication: _____

_____

_____

_____

_____

_____

_____

_____

_____

_____

_____

_____

_____

_____

_____

ic passage: _____

_____

_____

Cross-references:

Verse:	Reference:	Key thought:

fficulties:

Verse:	Question:

inent truth:_____

_____

_____

_____

_____

_____

_____

_____

Final study:

_____

_____

_____

_____

_____

_____

_____

_____

_____

_____

_____

_____

_____

_____

_____

_____

_____

_____

_____

_____

_____

_____

_____

_____

_____

_____

_____

_____

_____

COMPREHENSIVE BOOK ANALYSIS

BOOK SURVEY

Date: _____

Book: _____

Principal personalities: _____

_____

_____

Historical setting: _____

_____

_____

Purpose: _____

_____

_____

Themes: _____

_____

_____

Style: _____

Key words: _____

_____

Additional personalities: _____

_____

Geography: _____

_____

BOOK SURVEY

Overview:

_____

_____

_____

_____

_____

_____

_____

_____

_____

_____

_____

_____

_____

_____

_____

_____

_____

_____

_____

_____

_____

_____

CHAPTER ANALYSIS

Date: _____

Passage: _____

Passage description:

_____

_____

_____

_____

_____

_____

_____

_____

_____

_____

_____

_____

_____

_____

_____

_____

_____

_____

_____

_____

_____

_____

CHAPTER ANALYSIS

Verse:	Observations:	Verse:	Questions and answers

HAPTER ANALYSIS

Verse:	Cross-reference and linking thought	Notes and comments

CHAPTER ANALYSIS

Title: _____

Theme: _____

_____

_____

Conclusions: _____

_____

_____

_____

_____

_____

_____

Application: _____

_____

_____

_____

_____

_____

_____

_____

_____

_____

BOOK SUMMARY

Date: _____

Book: _____

Book title: _____

Final outline:

_____

_____

_____

_____

_____

_____

_____

_____

_____

_____

_____

_____

_____

_____

_____

_____

_____

_____

_____

_____

_____

_____

BOOK SUMMARY

Main themes:_____

_____

_____

_____

_____

Main conclusions:_____

_____

_____

_____

_____

_____

_____

_____

_____

_____

Final application:_____

_____

_____

_____

_____

_____

_____

_____

TOPICAL BIBLE STUDY

Date: _____

Topic: _____

Passages studied:

Reference:	Identifying thought:

Summary or outline:

_____

_____

_____

_____

_____

_____

_____

_____

_____

_____

_____

_____

_____

_____

_____

_____

_____

_____

_____

_____

_____

_____

_____

☐ Key verse or ☐ Favorite verse:

_____

_____

ıstrations:

_____

_____

_____

_____

oblems:

Reference:	Identifying question:

plication:_____

_____

_____

_____

_____

_____

_____

_____

BIBLE CHARACTER STUDY

Date: _____

Person studied: _____

Scriptures used:

Reference:	Key thought:

ographical sketch:

_____

_____

_____

_____

_____

_____

_____

_____

_____

_____

_____

_____

_____

ey verse:_____

_____

_____

ading lesson:_____

_____

_____

_____

_____

_____

_____

Problems:

Reference:	Identifying question:

Application:_____

_____

_____

_____

_____

_____

_____

_____